AF179748

HOUSING ISSUES, LAWS AND PROGRAMS

HOUSING FINANCE AND THE SECONDARY MORTGAGE MARKET

ALTERNATIVES FOR CHANGE

HOUSING ISSUES, LAWS AND PROGRAMS

Additional books in this series can be found on Nova's website under the Series tab.

Additional e-books in this series can be found on Nova's website under the e-book tab.

HOUSING ISSUES, LAWS AND PROGRAMS

HOUSING FINANCE AND THE SECONDARY MORTGAGE MARKET

ALTERNATIVES FOR CHANGE

SALLY G. MITCHELL
EDITOR

nova publishers
New York

Copyright © 2015 by Nova Science Publishers, Inc.

All rights reserved. No part of this book may be reproduced, stored in a retrieval system or transmitted in any form or by any means: electronic, electrostatic, magnetic, tape, mechanical photocopying, recording or otherwise without the written permission of the Publisher.

We have partnered with Copyright Clearance Center to make it easy for you to obtain permissions to reuse content from this publication. Simply navigate to this publication's page on Nova's website and locate the "Get Permission" button below the title description. This button is linked directly to the title's permission page on copyright.com. Alternatively, you can visit copyright.com and search by title, ISBN, or ISSN.

For further questions about using the service on copyright.com, please contact:
Copyright Clearance Center
Phone: +1-(978) 750-8400 Fax: +1-(978) 750-4470 E-mail: info@copyright.com.

NOTICE TO THE READER

The Publisher has taken reasonable care in the preparation of this book, but makes no expressed or implied warranty of any kind and assumes no responsibility for any errors or omissions. No liability is assumed for incidental or consequential damages in connection with or arising out of information contained in this book. The Publisher shall not be liable for any special, consequential, or exemplary damages resulting, in whole or in part, from the readers' use of, or reliance upon, this material. Any parts of this book based on government reports are so indicated and copyright is claimed for those parts to the extent applicable to compilations of such works.

Independent verification should be sought for any data, advice or recommendations contained in this book. In addition, no responsibility is assumed by the publisher for any injury and/or damage to persons or property arising from any methods, products, instructions, ideas or otherwise contained in this publication.

This publication is designed to provide accurate and authoritative information with regard to the subject matter covered herein. It is sold with the clear understanding that the Publisher is not engaged in rendering legal or any other professional services. If legal or any other expert assistance is required, the services of a competent person should be sought. FROM A DECLARATION OF PARTICIPANTS JOINTLY ADOPTED BY A COMMITTEE OF THE AMERICAN BAR ASSOCIATION AND A COMMITTEE OF PUBLISHERS.

Additional color graphics may be available in the e-book version of this book.

Library of Congress Cataloging-in-Publication Data

ISBN: 978-1-63482-877-2

Published by Nova Science Publishers, Inc. † New York

CONTENTS

PREFACE

This book serves as a primer that explains how the system of housing finance works. This book also examines various mechanisms that policymakers could use to attract more private capital to the secondary mortgage market; and addresses how those mechanisms could be combined in different ways to help the market make the transition to a new structure during the coming decade.

Chapter 1 – When making a decision about housing, a household must choose between renting and owning. Multiple factors, such as a household's financial status and expectations about the future, will influence the decision. Few that decide to purchase a home have the necessary savings or available financial resources to make the purchase on their own. Most need to take out a loan. A loan that uses real estate as collateral is typically referred to as a mortgage.

A potential borrower applies for a loan from a lender in what is called the primary market. The lender underwrites, or evaluates, the borrower and decides whether and under what terms to extend a loan. Different types of lenders make home loans, including banks, credit unions, and finance companies (institutions that lend money but do not accept deposits). The lender requires some additional assurance that, in the event that the borrower does not repay the mortgage as promised, it will be able to sell the home for enough to recoup the amount it is owed. Typically, lenders receive such assurance through a down payment, mortgage insurance, or a combination of the two. Mortgage insurance can be provided privately or through a government guarantee. If a mortgage is made, the borrower sends the required payments to an entity known as a mortgage servicer, which then remits the payments to the mortgage holder (the mortgage holder could be the original lender or, if the mortgage is sold, an investor). If the borrower does not repay the mortgage as promised, the lender can repossess the property through a process known as foreclosure.

The secondary market is the market for buying and selling mortgages. If a mortgage originator sells the mortgage in the secondary market, the purchaser of the mortgage could choose to hold the mortgage itself or to securitize it. When a mortgage is securitized, it is pooled into a security with other mortgages, and the payment streams associated with the mortgages are sold to investors. Fannie Mae and Freddie Mac securitize mortgages that conform to their standards, known as "conforming mortgages." Mortgages that do not conform to all of Fannie Mae's and Freddie Mac's standards are referred to as "nonconforming mortgages." Ginnie Mae guarantees mortgage-backed securities (MBS) made up exclusively of mortgages insured or guaranteed by the federal government. Other financial institutions also issue MBS, known as private-label securities (PLS). The characteristics of the borrower and of the mortgage determine the classification of the loan. What happens to a mortgage in the secondary market is partially determined by whether the mortgage is government-insured, conforming, or nonconforming. Depending on the type of MBS or mortgage purchased, investors will face different types of risks.

Congress is interested in the condition of the housing finance system for multiple reasons. The mortgage market is very large and can impact the wider U.S. economy. The federal government supports homeownership both directly (through the Federal Housing Administration [FHA], Department of Veterans' Affairs [VA], and U.S. Department of Agriculture [USDA]) and indirectly (through Fannie Mae and Freddie Mac). This support by the federal government means that the government is potentially liable for financial losses. Fannie Mae, Freddie Mac, and FHA currently are in financial difficulty, and Congress has shown an interest in exercising oversight and considering legislation to potentially address these difficulties and reform the broader system.

Chapter 2 – More than six years after the federal government took control of Fannie Mae and Freddie Mac, policy-makers are weighing a comprehensive overhaul of the mortgage finance system that could shrink or eventually close the two entities and create a system with more private capital. Fannie Mae and Freddie Mac were originally chartered as government-sponsored enterprises (GSEs) to ensure a stable supply of credit for residential mortgages nationwide. They operate in the secondary (or resale) market where they buy mortgages from the financial institutions that make the loans (thus ensuring that those institutions have a source of funds to originate new mortgages). Fannie Mae and

Freddie Mac then pool those loans to create mortgage-backed securities (MBSs), which they guarantee against defaults on principal and interest payments by borrowers and sell to investors.

Through its financial commitment to the two GSEs and its other mortgage programs, the federal government now directly or indirectly insures over 70 percent of all new residential mortgages. Loans guaranteed by Fannie Mae and Freddie Mac account for over two-thirds of those mortgages (about 50 percent of the total amount of mortgages), and loans insured by the Federal Housing Administration (FHA) make up most of the remaining federal share. Such government dominance was not always the case—in the 20 years before the financial crisis that began in 2007, roughly half of all mortgages were financed without backing from the federal government or either of the GSEs.

As the effects of the financial crisis have receded and as the housing market has recovered, policymakers have taken some initial steps toward returning to a secondary mortgage market with more private-sector involvement. Those steps include raising the fees that Fannie Mae and Freddie Mac charge for their guarantees to levels that private firms may be better able to compete with. The Congressional Budget Office (CBO) expects that the steps already taken, together with pending changes to financial regulations, will reduce the two GSEs' share of the mortgage market over the next 10 years.

This report examines various mechanisms that policy makers could use to attract more private capital to the secondary mortgage market. The report also addresses how those mechanisms could be combined in different ways to help the market make the transition to a new structure during the coming decade.

In: Housing Finance …
Editor: Sally G. Mitchell
ISBN: 978-1-63482-877-2
© 2015 Nova Science Publishers, Inc.

Chapter 1

An Overview of the Housing Finance System in the United States*

Sean M. Hoskins, Katie Jones and N. Eric Weiss

Summary

When making a decision about housing, a household must choose between renting and owning. Multiple factors, such as a household's financial status and expectations about the future, will influence the decision. Few that decide to purchase a home have the necessary savings or available financial resources to make the purchase on their own. Most need to take out a loan. A loan that uses real estate as collateral is typically referred to as a mortgage.

A potential borrower applies for a loan from a lender in what is called the primary market. The lender underwrites, or evaluates, the borrower and decides whether and under what terms to extend a loan. Different types of lenders make home loans, including banks, credit unions, and finance companies (institutions that lend money but do not accept deposits). The lender requires some additional assurance that, in the event that the borrower does not repay the mortgage as promised, it will be able to sell the home for enough to recoup the amount it is owed. Typically, lenders receive such assurance through a down payment, mortgage insurance, or a combination of the two. Mortgage insurance can

---

* This is an edited, reformatted and augmented version of a Congressional Research Service publication R42995, prepared for Members and Committees of Congress, dated February 19, 2015.

be provided privately or through a government guarantee. If a mortgage is made, the borrower sends the required payments to an entity known as a mortgage servicer, which then remits the payments to the mortgage holder (the mortgage holder could be the original lender or, if the mortgage is sold, an investor). If the borrower does not repay the mortgage as promised, the lender can repossess the property through a process known as foreclosure.

The secondary market is the market for buying and selling mortgages. If a mortgage originator sells the mortgage in the secondary market, the purchaser of the mortgage could choose to hold the mortgage itself or to securitize it. When a mortgage is securitized, it is pooled into a security with other mortgages, and the payment streams associated with the mortgages are sold to investors. Fannie Mae and Freddie Mac securitize mortgages that conform to their standards, known as "conforming mortgages." Mortgages that do not conform to all of Fannie Mae's and Freddie Mac's standards are referred to as "nonconforming mortgages." Ginnie Mae guarantees mortgage-backed securities (MBS) made up exclusively of mortgages insured or guaranteed by the federal government. Other financial institutions also issue MBS, known as private-label securities (PLS). The characteristics of the borrower and of the mortgage determine the classification of the loan. What happens to a mortgage in the secondary market is partially determined by whether the mortgage is government-insured, conforming, or nonconforming. Depending on the type of MBS or mortgage purchased, investors will face different types of risks.

Congress is interested in the condition of the housing finance system for multiple reasons. The mortgage market is very large and can impact the wider U.S. economy. The federal government supports homeownership both directly (through the Federal Housing Administration [FHA], Department of Veterans' Affairs [VA], and U.S. Department of Agriculture [USDA]) and indirectly (through Fannie Mae and Freddie Mac). This support by the federal government means that the government is potentially liable for financial losses. Fannie Mae, Freddie Mac, and FHA currently are in financial difficulty, and Congress has shown an interest in exercising oversight and considering legislation to potentially address these difficulties and reform the broader system.

INTRODUCTION

When making a decision about housing, a household often must evaluate renting versus owning. Multiple factors will influence the decision, such as a household's financial status and expectations about the future. Few that decide to purchase a home have the necessary savings or available financial resources to make the purchase without borrowing money. Most need to take out a loan known as a mortgage. This report serves as a primer that explains how the system of housing finance works. This report focuses on single-family, owner-occupied housing and not on commercial or multi-family real estate.[1]

Historically, the government has played an important role in the housing finance system, providing both support to the system and regulation of it. As is described in more detail later in this report, the government provides explicit support to certain homeowners, such as through government agencies like the Federal Housing Administration (FHA),[2] and implicit support to others, such as through the *government-sponsored enterprises* (GSEs) *Fannie Mae* and *Freddie Mac*. Advocates of government support for homeownership argue that homeownership strengthens ties to community and is a way for households to accumulate wealth. The government's support attempts to balance two competing objectives: expanding access to homeownership for qualified borrowers and minimizing the risk and cost to the government.

The government's regulation of the housing finance system is divided across the different levels of government. Some issues, such as the *foreclosure* process, are primarily regulated by the states, while other issues, such as certain borrower protections when taking out a mortgage, are regulated at the federal level. This report largely focuses on the federal role in supporting housing finance, not on its role in the regulation of it.

The housing finance system has two major components: a *primary market* and a *secondary market*. Lenders make new loans in the primary market, and loans are bought and sold in the secondary market. The next section will describe the primary market, explaining what a mortgage is and how a mortgage is made.

THE PRIMARY MARKET

In the primary market, a lender extends a loan to a borrower so that the borrower can purchase a house.[3] Many different types of lenders make home loans, including banks, credit unions, and finance companies (institutions that lend money but do not necessarily accept deposits). A loan that uses real estate as collateral is typically referred to as a *mortgage*. When a borrower applies for a mortgage, the lender will underwrite, or evaluate, the borrower.

The lender is likely to take into account multiple factors, such as the applicant's credit history, income, debts, assets, and the value of the house being purchased. The underwriting process usually takes several weeks or a month as the borrower assembles various financial documents, such as tax returns, that the lender requires.

The mortgage application process can be relatively expensive for borrowers. The borrower pays a variety of fees upfront for items such as credit reports, an independent appraisal, a survey of the land, a title search, and lender fees. The borrower generally has to pay additional costs when the mortgage is closed. Collectively, these are referred to as settlement costs or *closing costs*.[4] The borrower and the seller can negotiate who will pay which fees, but the borrower is generally responsible for at least some closing costs. The lender is required to provide a standardized form to the borrower at *closing* that shows the itemized closing costs associated with the mortgage.[5]

Mortgage Characteristics

A mortgage has four basic characteristics:[6]

- the amount of the loan (the principal);
- the length (or term) of the loan;
- the schedule for the loan's repayment (monthly installments or lump sum); and
- the interest rate.

Different types of mortgages vary across these characteristics. A *fixed-rate mortgage* is a mortgage in which the interest rate does not change over the life of the loan. An *adjustable-rate mortgage* has an interest rate that is tied to an underlying index; at agreed-upon intervals, as the index adjusts, so does the interest rate.[7] A balloon mortgage has a lump-sum amount, or a *balloon payment*, due at the end of the loan.

The most common type of mortgage in the United States is the 30-year, fixed-rate, *self-amortizing* mortgage. A self-amortizing mortgage is one in which each payment made by the borrower pays down some of the interest and some of the principal until the loan is paid off. For example, if a borrower takes out a $200,000 mortgage with a 6.5% fixed interest rate to be repaid over 30 years, then the borrower's monthly payment is about $1,264.[8] After 360 months of making monthly payments of $1,264 (one payment per month for 30 years), the mortgage is completely paid off. With adjustable-rate mortgages, the amount of the borrower's monthly payment can change as the interest rate adjusts.

Although the typical mortgage contract may have a 30-year term, most mortgages are paid off early. Borrowers pay off a mortgage in several ways. First, a borrower could repay the loan in full over the prescribed time period, or earlier if the borrower makes extra payments. Second, the borrower could *refinance* the mortgage. In a refinance, the borrower takes out a new mortgage (usually with better terms than the original, such as a lower interest rate)[9] and uses the new mortgage to repay the original mortgage. The borrower then makes payments on the new mortgage. Third, a borrower could sell the home and use the proceeds to repay the mortgage. Fourth, a borrower could stop paying, or *default*, on the mortgage. The lender would then repossess the house through foreclosure and sell it to attempt to recoup the unpaid amount of the loan.

Lender Protection

When taking out a mortgage, the house that is being purchased is pledged as collateral. If the borrower is unable or unwilling to pay, the lender can seize the house and sell it to recoup what is owed.[10] To increase the probability that the sale of the house will be sufficient to recover the amount of the mortgage outstanding, the lender will generally require a *down payment*. The down payment serves as a buffer to protect the lender in the event that house prices fall. For example, if a borrower wants to purchase a $200,000 house,[11] the lender may require the borrower to provide a 20% down payment ($40,000) in order to borrow the additional $160,000.[12] As long as the house can be sold for more than the amount of the mortgage outstanding, the lender faces little risk of not being repaid. A larger down payment results in a lower *loan-to-value ratio*, or the ratio of the amount of the mortgage to the value of the home.

Lenders typically require a borrower to have a 20% down payment. If a borrower does not have the necessary down payment, the borrower has several options. One potential option is for a borrower to take out a second mortgage (or a "piggyback loan") to help finance the down payment. For example, a borrower could put down 10% of the value of the house, borrow 10% as a piggyback loan (which is combined with the 10% to serve as the down payment), and then borrow the remaining 80% as the first mortgage. The first mortgage is said to be first because, in the event the borrower goes into foreclosure, the first mortgage is supposed to be repaid first from the proceeds of selling the house. To compensate for the additional risk of being second in the repayment order, the second mortgage usually charges a higher interest rate than the first mortgage.

A borrower could also use mortgage insurance if he or she does not have enough for a 20% down payment. Mortgage insurance, which is an insurance policy that can be purchased by either the borrower or the lender (though usually by the borrower), compensates the lender in the event that the borrower defaults. Mortgage insurance provides greater assurance to the lender that the lender will be repaid. Mortgage insurance is typically purchased by borrowers from private businesses (*private mortgage insurance* or PMI) or the federal government.

Government mortgage insurance coverage varies depending on the agency providing the insurance, but most programs require low or no down payment. The three main agencies that provide government mortgage insurance are the following:

- *Federal Housing Administration (FHA).*[13] FHA, an agency within the Department of Housing and Urban Development (HUD), provides mortgage insurance on loans that meet its requirements (including a minimum down payment requirement and an initial *principal balance* below a certain threshold) in exchange for fees, or premiums, paid by borrowers. If a borrower defaults on an FHA-insured mortgage, FHA will repay the lender the entire remaining principal amount it is owed. FHA is the largest provider of government mortgage insurance.
- *Department of Veterans Affairs (VA).*[14] VA provides a guaranty on certain mortgages made to veterans. If a borrower defaults on a VA-guaranteed mortgage, the VA will repay the lender a portion (but not all) of the remaining principal amount owed. Because it is limited to veterans, the VA loan guaranty program is smaller and more narrowly targeted than FHA.
- *U.S. Department of Agriculture (USDA).*[15] USDA administers a direct loan program for low-income borrowers in rural areas, and a loan guarantee program for low- and moderate-income borrowers in rural areas. If a borrower defaults on a USDA-insured loan, USDA repays the lender a portion (but not all) of the remaining principal amount owed. The USDA program is more narrowly targeted than FHA in that it has income limits and is limited to rural areas.

In recent years, there has been much concern about FHA's financial status, most recently stemming from an actuarial report estimating that FHA does not currently have enough funds on hand to cover all of its anticipated future losses.

Mortgage Servicing

After a loan is made, the borrower is responsible for making the required payments on the mortgage. In the housing finance system, a mortgage *servicer* is usually hired by the lender to function as the intermediary between the lender[16] and the borrower. The role of the servicer may be performed by the same institution that made the loan to the borrower, or the servicing could be performed by another institution.

When a borrower is current (making the required payments on time), a mortgage servicer collects payments from the borrower and forwards them to the lender.[17] If the borrower is behind on the payments (i.e., is *delinquent*), the servicer may offer the borrower a workout option to potentially allow the borrower to stay in his or her home. Examples of workout options include loan modifications, such as principal balance reductions and interest rate reductions, as well as repayments plans, which allow borrowers to repay the amounts they owe over a period of time to become current on their mortgage payments. If the borrower is in *default*, which can be defined in different ways but generally means that the borrower has missed a certain number of mortgage payments, the servicer may pursue a mortgage liquidation option. Mortgage liquidation options include foreclosure as well as a *short sale*, a process in which the borrower sells the home and uses the proceeds to satisfy the mortgage debt even if the sale proceeds are less than the amount owed on the mortgage.[18]

Mortgage Classifications

Mortgages can be classified into several categories based on their characteristics. The broadest distinction is between *government-insured mortgages* and *conventional mortgages*. Government-insured mortgages have mortgage insurance from a government agency, such as FHA, whereas conventional mortgages do not have government insurance. As noted, this insurance pays the lender if the borrower defaults. Borrowers can also be classified into two broad groups based on their credit history: *prime* and *non-prime*. Although there is no single agreed-upon definition, prime borrowers generally have very good credit and are offered more attractive mortgage terms, such as better interest rates, than non-prime borrowers. Non-prime borrowers exhibit one or more factors that make them appear riskier to lenders, such as past credit problems or a lack of complete income and asset documentation.

Conventional mortgages can be broken down into two additional groups, *conforming* and *nonconforming* mortgages. Conforming loans are loans that are eligible to be purchased in the secondary market by Fannie Mae and Freddie Mac, two GSEs that are discussed later in this report. To be a conforming loan, the mortgage must meet certain creditworthiness thresholds (such as a minimum *credit score*) and be below the "conforming loan limit," a legal cap on the principal balance of the mortgage that can vary based on the geographic area where the house is located.[19] Borrowers with conforming loans are usually prime borrowers.

Nonconforming loans can be broken down into three additional categories. First, nonconforming loans that are above the conforming loan limit are called *jumbo loans*.[20] Second, *Alt-A loans* are for near-prime borrowers who may have credit problems or who do not have complete documentation for income or assets. Third, *subprime loans* are generally for the riskiest borrowers; they either have low credit scores, documentation issues, or some other factor that makes them appear to be riskier to lenders. Subprime borrowers are likely to be charged a higher interest rate to compensate the lender for the additional risk.[21]

Risks Associated with Holding Mortgages

When a lender originates a mortgage, it accepts certain risks. The three major risks are credit, prepayment, and funding risk.

Credit risk refers to the risk that the lender[22] bears if a borrower does not repay the mortgage on time. *Prepayment risk* is the risk that a mortgage will be paid off sooner than expected, typically by a borrower refinancing the mortgage or selling the home. This is more likely to happen when interest rates fall.[23] When interest rates fall, borrowers are more likely to refinance their mortgages to take advantage of lower interest rates. When a borrower refinances, the lender is repaid the amount that it is still owed, but it now has to reinvest those funds at a time when its expected return on new investments is lower because interest rates have fallen.

Although prepayment risk is a risk associated with falling interest rates, there are also risks for lenders that come from rising interest rates. One of these risks, called *funding risk*, arises because some lenders borrow money in the short term to fund long-term investments, such as 30-year mortgages. Short-term interest rates are typically lower than long-term interest rates because of the additional risk associated with lending money for a longer period of time. Lenders, therefore, can profit off of the difference, or spread, between the short-term and long-term rates. If interest rates rise, then the lender will have to borrow funds at a higher interest rate, while still earning the same interest rate on the mortgage. As long as the short-term rate stays below the long-term return, the lender would profit on the difference, although its profits would be lower than if the short-term interest rates had not increased. If short-term rates increase above the fixed return on the mortgage, then the investment would no longer be profitable.

Rising interest rates also present opportunity costs for lenders. If interest rates rise, but lenders' money is tied up in long-term mortgages made at lower interest rates, then the lender is missing out on higher returns that it could be earning if it were able to originate mortgages or make other investments at the higher current interest rate.

The lender that originates a mortgage does not necessarily have to bear all of the risks associated with that mortgage. In some cases, the borrower could bear some of these risks. Adjustable-rate mortgages, for example, transfer the risk that interest rates might rise from the lender to the borrower. Lenders can also sell mortgages to investors, who will then bear the risks associated with the mortgage. The market for buying and selling mortgages is called the secondary market, and it is described in the next section.

Primary Market Summary

A potential borrower applies for a loan from a lender in the primary market. The lender evaluates the borrower and decides whether to extend a loan and on what terms. The lender typically requires some additional assurance that the loan will be repaid either through a down payment or mortgage insurance (or a combination of the two). If the loan is made, the borrower sends the required scheduled payments to the servicer, which then remits the payments to the mortgage holder. The characteristics of the borrower and of the mortgage determine the classification of the loan. As is discussed next in "The Secondary Market" section, what happens to a mortgage in the secondary market is partially determined by whether the mortgage is government-insured, conforming, or nonconforming.

THE SECONDARY MARKET

After a lender originates a mortgage loan, the lender has several options. The lender could choose to hold the mortgage in its *portfolio* and not sell it. The lender could also choose to sell the mortgage to another entity. Mortgages are bought and sold in the *secondary market* to domestic and international investors. If the mortgage is sold, the borrower would continue to send monthly mortgage payments to the mortgage servicer, which could be the original lender or a new entity.[24]

The secondary market plays an important role in providing funding for the loans made in the primary market. When a mortgage is sold in the secondary market, the lender can use the proceeds to fund additional new mortgages in the primary market. If the lender holds the mortgage in its portfolio, the lender has fewer available funds to make new mortgages. Furthermore, selling the loan to another entity allows the lender to transfer the risks associated with mortgage lending to the buyer of the mortgage.

Securitization

When a lender chooses to sell a mortgage in the secondary market, the new mortgage holder could choose to hold the mortgage as a *whole loan*. When held as a whole loan, the mortgage is in the portfolio of the new mortgage holder just as it was in the portfolio of the lender, and the new mortgage holder would bear the risks associated with the mortgage.[25] Instead of holding the mortgage as a whole loan, the new mortgage holder could also choose to *securitize* the mortgage.

Mortgage securitization comes in many different forms, but generally speaking, the process involves a financial institution acquiring and pooling together many different mortgages and then issuing a *mortgage-backed security* (MBS). An MBS could be divided up into different pieces, or *tranches*, that are sold to investors.[26] The investors do not own the underlying mortgages but are buying the right to receive the future stream of payments that come from those mortgages. A servicer collects the payments of all the borrowers whose mortgages are part of the security and remits the payments to the investors.

For investors, purchasing an MBS offers several benefits compared with holding whole mortgages. Most notably, an MBS is generally more *liquid* than whole mortgages, meaning it is easier to quickly sell an MBS at the current price. Because the market for MBS is more liquid than the market for whole mortgages, MBS might be attractive to investors who would not otherwise choose to invest in mortgages. More investors in the mortgage market, in turn, can mean more funding is available for lenders to offer mortgages. More funding available in the primary market and the existence of a secondary market where lenders know that they can easily sell the mortgages that they make can result in lower interest rates that lenders charge to borrowers.

Although securitization may have several advantages, it may also present several disadvantages. Securitization—and the secondary market in general—includes more participants in facilitating the flow of credit than when a loan is held by the originator. Additional participants, with some acting on behalf of others, can introduce competing incentives for the various participants and potential conflicts of interest. For example, more participants in the transaction may result in a principal-agent problem, a situation in which one entity (the agent) is supposed to work on behalf of another entity (the principal), but the agent may have an incentive to act in its own best interest rather than in the best interest of the principal. For example, mortgage servicers act on behalf of investors to evaluate a borrower for mortgage workout options or to begin the foreclosure process when a borrower falls behind on mortgage payments, as specified by a contract between the investor and the servicer. However, in some cases, a servicer may have an incentive to choose the option that is in its own best interest rather than in the best interest of the investor, and the investor might not be well positioned to police the servicer's actions.[27]

Figure 1 is a simplified model showing the housing finance system when mortgages are securitized. The lines in the figure represent relationships between the different entities involved, and generally involve money flowing in one or both directions. In the scenario shown in the figure, borrowers receive money to buy homes through mortgages made by loan originators. The originators then sell the mortgages to a securitizer, who in turn sells pools of mortgages to investors as MBS. The borrower sends monthly mortgage payments to a mortgage servicer, who passes those payments on to the investors (and to any other entities who are owed part of the payment, such as tax or insurance payments). Investors, in turn, pay the mortgage servicer a fee for servicing the mortgage. Alternatively, it is possible that the originator of the mortgage will hold that mortgage itself, or that it will sell it to another entity that will hold the whole mortgage rather than securitize it. In such cases, which are not represented in the figure, the securitizer and investors would not be involved. The servicer would send the borrower's monthly mortgage payments to whoever holds the mortgage, whether that is the originator or another entity.

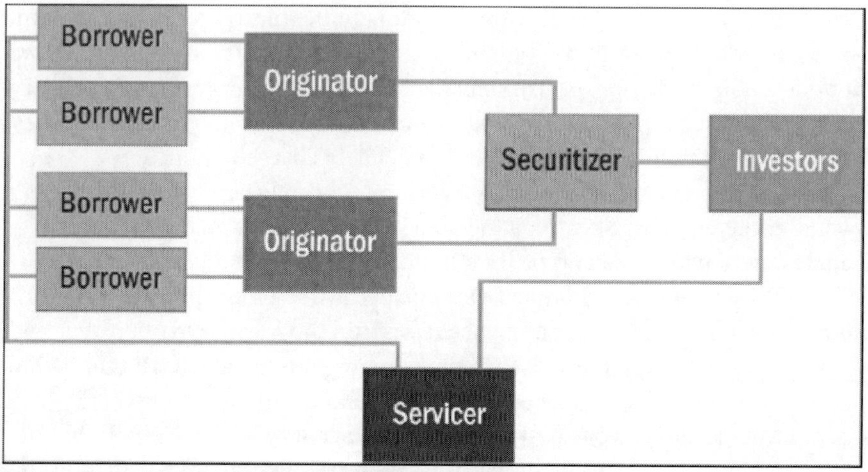

Source: Created by the Congressional Research Service (CRS).

Note: In this simplified illustration of the housing finance system when a mortgage is securitized, borrowers receive mortgages from originators, and the originators then sell those mortgages to securitizers to be pooled into MBS. Investors, in turn, buy the payment streams associated with the mortgages underlying the MBS. A mortgage servicer collects monthly mortgage payments from the borrower and forwards them to the investors. The investors pay a fee to the servicer for servicing the mortgage.

Figure 1. The Housing Finance System When a Mortgage is Securitized.

Types of MBS

The securitization process can take many different forms, but there are three broad categories that are described below: Fannie Mae and Freddie Mac, Ginnie Mae, and *private-label securitization* (PLS). The underlying loans that comprise the MBS are related to the mortgage classifications described in "The Primary Market" section of this report: generally, conforming mortgages are included in Fannie Mae and Freddie Mac MBS, government-insured mortgages in Ginnie Mae MBS, and nonconforming mortgages in private-label MBS, though there are exceptions.[28]

When mortgages are securitized, investors generally take on the risks associated with the mortgage loan, such as credit risk and prepayment risk. However, in some cases, another entity might guarantee the MBS, in which case the entity providing the guaranty takes on the credit risk while investors bear the risks associated with rising and falling interest rates. Investors in Fannie Mae, Freddie Mac, and Ginnie Mae MBS do not bear credit risk because of the guarantees those entities provide, but investors in PLS and holders of non-guaranteed mortgages may be exposed to credit risk.

Fannie Mae and Freddie Mac

During the Great Depression, Congress created Fannie Mae (officially, the Federal National Mortgage Association, or FNMA) as a government agency to encourage mortgage lending.[29] In 1968, Congress divided Fannie Mae into two parts: (1) a government corporation, the Government National Mortgage Association or Ginnie Mae (described below) and (2) a government-sponsored enterprise (GSE) that retained the name Fannie Mae. In 1970, Congress established Freddie Mac (Federal Home Loan Mortgage Corporation) as part of the *Federal Home Loan Bank System* and owned by member banks.

Fannie Mae and Freddie Mac do not originate mortgages, a process that occurs in the primary market. Instead, the GSEs purchase conforming mortgages—mortgages that meet their eligibility criteria. The GSEs either hold the mortgages in their own portfolios or pool the mortgages into MBS, which are sold to investors or retained by the GSEs as investments. The GSEs guarantee that investors in these MBS will receive timely payment of principal and interest even if the borrower becomes delinquent. The GSE guarantee transfers the credit risk (the risk that some borrowers might default and not repay their mortgages) from the investors to the GSEs. To compensate the GSEs for their guarantee, the GSEs receive a *guarantee fee*. The GSE guarantee makes their MBS more easily traded and worth more to investors, increasing their demand for MBS. The support provided by the GSEs in the secondary market can translate to lower rates for borrowers in the primary market.[30]

Both Fannie Mae and Freddie Mac are private companies, though both have congressional charters that contain special privileges and certain special responsibilities to support affordable housing for low- and moderate-income households. As private companies, their employees are not government employees, and their debts are explicitly not backed by the federal government.

Despite the explicit disclaimer, it has been commonly believed that the federal government would, in fact, back the GSEs. In September 2008, Fannie Mae and Freddie Mac were in extreme financial difficulty and agreed to be placed in voluntary *conservatorship*, which allows the federal government to run them. The stated goal of the conservatorship is to conserve the enterprises' assets and to eventually return them to stockholder control.[31]

Ginnie Mae

Congress established Ginnie Mae in 1968 when it divided Fannie Mae into two separate entities. Ginnie Mae remains a government agency as part of the Department of Housing and Urban Development.

Ginnie Mae guarantees MBS made up exclusively of mortgages insured or guaranteed by the federal government, namely FHA, VA, USDA, or HUD's Office of Public and Indian Housing. Similar to the GSEs, Ginnie Mae guarantees investors in its MBS timely payment of principal and interest payments in exchange for a guarantee fee. By providing a secondary market for government-backed mortgages, Ginnie Mae increases the amount of capital available in the primary market for lenders to offer government-backed mortgages. Unlike Fannie Mae and Freddie Mac, Ginnie Mae does not purchase or securitize mortgages; rather, it guarantees the MBS issued by certain issuers (such as banks or credit unions) that have been approved by Ginnie Mae. Furthermore, Ginnie Mae's employees are government employees, and its guaranty is explicitly backed by the full faith and credit of the U.S. government. This means that, if Ginnie Mae were unable to fulfill its obligations, investors in its MBS would be paid with funds from the U.S. Treasury because the guaranty is explicitly backed by the federal government.

Private-Label Securities

Private-label securitization (PLS) is a form of securitization that typically uses nonconforming mortgages, meaning mortgages that do not conform to the GSE standards either because they are too large (jumbo loans) or because they do not meet the necessary credit standards (typically these loans will be Alt-A and subprime). PLS is similar to GSE and Ginnie Mae securitization— both involve the pooling of mortgages and the issuing of securities—but PLS securities do not have an explicit or implicit government guarantee.

Unlike with PLS, GSE and Ginnie Mae securities provide a guarantee that minimizes the credit risk for the investor. PLS MBS instead often rely on alternative forms of "credit enhancement" to minimize the credit risk for investors. For example, a private-label MBS may purchase insurance[32] from a private insurer to guarantee payment for investors. Alternatively, the credit risk could be minimized for some investors by structuring the MBS so that there are multiple tranches, with the most senior tranche entitled to the first stream of payments that borrowers make (and assuming the least amount of risk) and the lowest tranche entitled to the remaining payments (and assuming the most risk).

In addition to MBS, there are other types of products that private-label securitizers create that are derived from mortgages. For example, instead of pooling together mortgages to issue an MBS, a securitizer could pool together different tranches of MBS as a *collateralized-debt obligation* (CDO).[33] Securitizers could also pool together CDOs to create even more types of products.

Table 1 summarizes the relationship between the different types of MBS and the different classifications of mortgages

Table 1. Mortgage-Backed Securities Classification

Type of MBS	Type of Underlying Mortgage
Fannie Mae and Freddie Mac	Conforming mortgages
Ginnie Mae	Government-guaranteed mortgages
Private Label	Conventional, nonconforming (jumbo, Alt-A, and subprime) mortgages

Source: Created by the Congressional Research Service (CRS).

Notes: The table shows the types of underlying mortgages that typically comprise the different types of MBS. By law, Ginnie Mae MBS can only contain federally insured mortgages. By law, Fannie Mae and Freddie Mac can only purchase conforming mortgages, and they have not found it profitable to purchase and securitize government-insured mortgages. Because of their GSE status, Fannie Mae and Freddie Mac have been able to offer better prices in the secondary mortgage market for conforming mortgages. Private-label securitizers have not been able to compete with the GSEs in issuing MBS backed by conforming mortgages.

Investors

Investors that purchase mortgages and MBS are an important source of funding for the mortgages originated in the primary market. Investors in MBS are typically large *institutional investors*, such as pension funds, domestic banks, foreign banks, and hedge funds. Investors choose which of the types of MBS to purchase based on the type and amount of risk the investor wishes to bear and on the expected return from their investment.

GSE, Ginnie Mae, and PLS MBS are generally divided into two broad categories: *agency MBS*, which includes GSE and Ginnie Mae MBS, and *non-agency MBS*, which is only PLS. Investors purchase agency and non-agency MBS in different ways.

To-Be-Announced Market

Agency MBS are typically purchased by investors through the *to-be-announced (TBA) market*. The TBA market is a forward market: the specific mortgages in the MBS that are being purchased are unknown on the date the trade is agreed to. Instead, the buyer and seller agree on several basic criteria[34] and the trade may not be settled (or completed) for several weeks. Two days before the trade is settled, the seller informs the buyer about the specifics of the pool being sold. The pool being sold must satisfy the original criteria agreed to in accordance with the settlement guidelines established by the Securities Industry and Financial Markets Association (SIFMA), an industry trade group.[35]

The TBA market provides several different benefits to the housing finance system. The establishment of a large and liquid secondary market can boost the demand for MBS by investors, which in turn can lower the interest rate charged to borrowers in the primary market.[36] In addition, by providing several weeks between when a trade is agreed to and eventually settled, the TBA market allows sellers of MBS to know the price and amount of MBS that they will sell at a future date. This can reduce the uncertainty they face in determining how many new mortgages to purchase or originate in the primary market and at what price. The time between when a trade is agreed to and when it is settled also helps borrowers to lock in interest rates a month or more before their loan is finalized.

Specified-Pool Market

Non-agency MBS are issued and sold by private companies to investors. They are ineligible for the TBA market and instead sell through a *specified-pool market* in which the details of the specific bonds are known when a trade is made.[37] Some agency MBS also sell in a specified-pool market, though most trade through the TBA market. Non-agency MBS tend to be less liquid than agency MBS, meaning it is more difficult to sell non-agency MBS without reducing the price. The relative illiquidity of specified-pool markets compared with the TBA market may be due to the structure of the market, the absence of a large forward market for non-agency MBS, or due to the type of securities that are being traded, securities that do not have a perceived or explicit government guarantee.

Secondary Market Summary

The secondary market is the market for buying and selling mortgages. Lenders might choose to keep the mortgages that they originate in their own portfolios, or they might sell them to the secondary market. If a mortgage originator sells the mortgage in the secondary mortgage, the purchaser of the mortgage could choose to hold the mortgage itself or to securitize it in a pool of mortgages. Fannie Mae and Freddie Mac securitize mortgages that conform to their criteria. Ginnie Mae guarantees MBS made up exclusively of mortgages insured or guaranteed by the federal government. Other financial institutions issue PLS that do not have an implicit or explicit government guarantee. Depending on the type of MBS or mortgage purchased, investors will face different types of risks, including credit risk and prepayment risk.

APPENDIX. GLOSSARY

Term	Definition
Adjustable-rate mortgage	An adjustable-rate mortgage is a mortgage where the interest rate can change at agreed-upon intervals (frequently annual) based on changes in a specified index.
Agency MBS	Agency MBS is a term used to refer to mortgage-backed securities that are guaranteed by Fannie Mae, Freddie Mac, or Ginnie Mae.
Alt-A mortgage	An Alt-A mortgage is a mortgage that is made to a borrower who is slightly less creditworthy than a prime borrower. This could be because of the borrower's credit rating or because less than standard documentation is provided.

Glossary (Continued)

Term	Definition
Amortization or amortization schedule	Amortization is the repayment of principal (as opposed to interest) on a loan. This determines how much of the original amount borrowed is owed at any time.
Balloon payment	A balloon payment is a special payment, usually larger than a standard monthly payment, at the end of a mortgage.
Basis point	A basis point is one-hundredth of one percentage point (0.01%). Basis point is sometimes shortened to point.
Closing	Closing is when loan documents are signed and the borrower is given the funds. In addition to the loan, documents transferring and registering the new ownership of a home are signed.
Closing costs	Closing costs are charged at the time loan documents are signed, which is called a closing. Closing costs can include legal fees and various taxes. In addition, borrowers are usually required to prepay certain costs, such as accrued property taxes, at closing.
Closing points	Closing points are a fee charged at the closing of a mortgage. The fee is stated in basis points and goes to the lender.
Collateralized debt obligation (CDO)	A CDO is a security created by mortgage securitizers that pools together different tranches of MBS.
Conforming loan limit	The conforming loan limit is the maximum original principal balance of a mortgage that can be purchased by Fannie Mae or Freddie Mac.
Conforming mortgage	A conforming mortgage meets the credit and loan limit standards for mortgages that Fannie Mae and Freddie Mac can purchase.
Conservatorship	Conservatorship is when management of a financial institution that is in financial trouble is taken over by an outside conservator. The goal of conservatorship is to return the institution to

Term	Definition
	stockholder control. The institution is placed in receivership and dissolved when it cannot recover financial health.
Conventional mortgage	A conventional mortgage is a mortgage that is not insured or guaranteed by a government agency, such as FHA, VA, or USDA.
Correspondent lenders	Correspondent lenders have a contractual relationship to sell loans, including mortgages, to another, usually larger, financial institution.
Credit risk	Credit risk is the risk to the mortgage holder that a borrower will default on the mortgage and not repay the loan as promised. This is sometimes also referred to as default risk.
Credit score	A credit score is a numerical evaluation of a borrower's credit history.
Department of Housing and Urban Development	The Department of Housing and Urban Development is a Cabinet-level agency that includes both the Federal Housing Administration (FHA) and Ginnie Mae.
Default	Default is the failure to meet contracted loan obligations, such as the failure to make monthly payments on time. Some use default to mean a borrower has missed three or more monthly loan payments. Others use default to mean a borrower has missed one monthly loan payment or other required action.
Delinquent	A delinquent borrower is not meeting contractual loan obligations such as to make monthly payments, but the failure to meet contractual obligations has not gone on long enough for the borrower to be considered to be in default. A borrower is generally considered to be delinquent as soon as he misses a mortgage payment.
Down payment	A down payment is money that the borrower puts towards the purchase of the home so that the entire cost of the home is not financed by the mortgage. Lenders generally require down payments to increase the probability that, if the borrower does

Glossary (Continued)

Term	Definition
	not repay the mortgage as promised, the home can be sold for an amount high enough to cover the mortgage amount outstanding.
Fannie Mae	Fannie Mae is a stockholder-owned company with a congressional charter that purchases already made mortgages. Its formal name is the Federal National Mortgage Association. Fannie Mae and Freddie Mac compete with each other.
Federal Home Loan Bank System	The Federal Home Loan Bank System is owned by member lenders and is chartered by Congress to provide liquidity to the mortgage market by lending funds using mortgages as collateral.
Federal Housing Administration (FHA)	The Federal Housing Administration (FHA) is a government agency with the Department of Housing and Urban Development that provides mortgage insurance on certain mortgages that meet its criteria and are made by private lenders.
Federal Housing Finance Agency (FHFA)	The Federal Housing Finance Agency (FHFA) is Fannie Mae's and Freddie Mac's regulator and conservator. FHFA also regulates the Federal Home Loan Bank System.
FICO	FICO scores are a credit score developed and calculated by a company of the same name.
Fixed-rate mortgage	A fixed-rate mortgage is a mortgage where the interest rate cannot change over the life of the mortgage. This is in contrast to an adjustable-rate mortgage.
Foreclosure	Foreclosure is the process by which a lender repossesses a home after a borrower defaults on the mortgage, or the outcome of that process. Laws governing foreclosure vary by state.
Freddie Mac	Freddie Mac is a stockholder-owned company with a congressional charter that purchases already made mortgages. Its formal name is the Federal Home Loan Mortgage Corporation. Freddie Mac and

Term	Definition
	Fannie Mae compete with each other.
Funding risk	Funding risk is the risk to mortgage holders that rising interest rates will decrease their profits. This could happen if mortgage holders borrow money in the short term and invest it in long-term investments, such as mortgages, to profit from the spread between short-term and long-term interest rates. If interest rates rise, the mortgage holder's borrowing costs go up, but the interest rate that it earns on its investments remains the same, reducing its profits.
Guarantee fee (G fee)	A G fee, or guarantee fee, is a fee that Fannie Mae and Freddie Mac charge the seller when they purchase a mortgage. The G fee is mandatory and is used to guarantee timely payment of principal and interest to whoever purchases the mortgage from Fannie Mae or Freddie Mac. Ginnie Mae also charges guarantee fees.
Ginnie Mae	Ginnie Mae, officially the Government National Mortgage Association, is a government agency that guarantees mortgage-backed securities that are made up of government-insured mortgages. The Ginnie Mae guarantee has the full faith and credit of the United States government behind it. Ginnie Mae is part of the Department of Housing and Urban Development.
Government-insured mortgage	A government-insured mortgage is a mortgage that is insured or guaranteed by a government agency, such as FHA, VA, or the USDA.
Government-sponsored enterprise (GSE)	A government-sponsored enterprise is a private company with a congressional charter, such as Fannie Mae and Freddie Mac. The Federal Home Loan Bank System is also a GSE.
Institutional investor	An institutional investor is an organization such as a commercial bank, sovereign wealth fund, college endowment, pension fund, or private equity fund that has large amounts of money to invest.

Glossary (Continued)

Term	Definition
Insured depository	An insured depository takes deposits that are insured. Commercial banks and credit unions are two types of insured depositories.
Interest rate risk	Interest rate risk is the risk that a mortgage holder could lose money on a mortgage due to changes in interest rates.
Jumbo loan	A jumbo loan is a loan where the original principal balance exceeds the maximum amount of a loan that Fannie Mae or Freddie Mac can purchase.
Liquid	Liquid is a term used to refer to markets where a commodity, such as mortgages, can be sold easily and quickly.
Loan-to-value ratio (LTV)	The loan-to-value ratio is the ratio of the principal balance of a mortgage to the value of the home that is used as collateral. A higher LTV means that a borrower has less equity in the home, and a low LTV means that a borrower has more equity in the home. LTVs are expressed as a percentage, such as 80%.
Mortgage	A mortgage is a loan with specific real estate as collateral.
Mortgage banker	A mortgage bank specializes in originating mortgages using its funds.
Mortgage broker	A mortgage broker brings a mortgage lender and a borrower together. The lender and the borrower might not actually meet.
Mortgage-backed security (MBS)	A mortgage-backed security is a bond that is collateralized by mortgages.
Non-agency MBS	Non-agency MBS is a term used to refer to private-label securities, that is, mortgage-backed securities that are issued by private companies and are not guaranteed by Fannie Mae, Freddie Mac, or Ginnie Mae.
Nonconforming mortgage	A nonconforming mortgage is a mortgage that does not meet the required criteria to be eligible to be purchased by Fannie Mae or Freddie Mac in the

Term	Definition
	secondary market.
Non-prime mortgage	A non-prime mortgage is a mortgage that does not qualify for the best mortgage terms, such as the lowest available interest rate, because the borrower has one or more factors that make him appear riskier to lenders. Alt-A mortgages and subprime mortgages are examples of non-prime mortgages.
Portfolio	A portfolio or investment portfolio is the financial assets (bonds, stocks, mortgage-backed securities, mutual funds, etc.) that an investor owns.
Portfolio lender	A portfolio lender makes mortgages that it intends to keep in its portfolio as investments.
Prepayment risk	Prepayment risk is the risk that a borrower will pay his mortgage earlier than anticipated, usually through refinancing. Since borrowers tend to refinance when interest rates decline, prepayments mean that a mortgage holder is unlikely to be able to reinvest the funds for as high of an interest rate as it was earning previously.
Primary mortgage market	The primary mortgage market is the market where lenders make mortgage loans to borrowers. It is not a physical location.
Prime mortgage	A prime mortgage is a mortgage made to a borrower with very good credit. The definition is somewhat vague and has varied over time.
Principal balance	The principal balance is the amount owed on a loan such as a mortgage.
Private-label securities	Private-label securities are securities that are issued by private companies are not guaranteed by Fannie Mae, Freddie Mac, or Ginnie Mae. Private-label securities are usually made up of nonconforming conventional mortgages, and do not provide a guarantee of timely payment of principal and interest payments for the investor in the case of a borrower defaulting on the mortgage.
Private mortgage insurance (PMI)	Private mortgage insurance (PMI) is typically required by lenders when a borrower does not make a 20% down payment. In the event of foreclosure,

Glossary (Continued)

Term	Definition
	PMI covers part of the lender's loss.
Receivership	Receivership is when a court or government regulator orders a financial company in severe distress dissolved to pay its creditors.
Refinance	A refinance is a transaction in which a borrower with an existing mortgage takes out a new mortgage (usually with better terms than the original, such as a lower interest rate) and uses the proceeds from the new mortgage to repay the original mortgage. The borrower then makes payments on the new mortgage.
Secondary mortgage market	The secondary mortgage market is where lenders and investors buy and sell loans. It is not a physical location.
Securitization	Securitization is the practice of pooling together many loans, such as mortgages, and selling the rights to receive the future stream of payments made on those loans to investors.
Self-amortizing mortgage	A self-amortizing mortgage is a mortgage where each payment made by the borrower pays off some of the principal mortgage amount and some of the interest until the mortgage is paid off.
Servicer	The servicer on a loan collects payments from the borrower and distributes the proceeds to the lender(s) and others (such as local property tax offices) entitled to payments.
Short sale	A short sale is an alternative to foreclosure where a borrower sells the home for less than the outstanding amount owed on the mortgage, and the lender accepts the sales proceeds as payment on a mortgage. Often, the lender will forgive the amount owed on the mortgage that exceeds the sales price, but it is possible for the borrower to still owe that amount in some cases. A lender agrees to a short sale because he is likely to receive more than in foreclosure.

Term	Definition
Specified-pool market	A specified pool market is a market for selling mortgage-backed securities in which the details of the specific mortgages that will be included in the security are known when the sale is made. Private-label securities are most likely to trade in a specified-pool market.
Subprime mortgage	Technically, a subprime mortgage is a mortgage to a borrower with less than a prime credit history. Alt-A mortgages come between prime and subprime mortgages. The term is also used to mean a mortgage with consumer unfriendly terms made to anyone.
To-be-announced (TBA) market	The to-be-announced market is a market for selling mortgage-backed securities in which the details of the specific mortgages that will be included in the security are not specified when the sale is made, but rather the buyer and seller agree to certain basic characteristics of the mortgages that will be included. Only Fannie Mae, Freddie Mac, and Ginnie Mae mortgage-backed securities trade in the to- be-announced market.
Tranche	A tranche is a piece or slice of a mortgage-backed security. Investors in different tranches of an MBS have different claims on the payment streams from the underlying mortgages.
USDA	The U.S. Department of Agriculture or USDA is a Cabinet-level agency that provides guarantees on mortgage loans made by private lenders to certain borrowers in rural areas.
VA	The Department of Veteran's Affairs or VA is a Cabinet-level agency that provides guarantees on mortgage loans made by private lenders to certain borrowers who are veterans.
Whole loan	A whole loan is a mortgage that is held as-is in the portfolio of a lender or another entity, rather than being pooled into a mortgage-backed security.

End Notes

[1] For more on commercial and multi-family real estate, see CRS Report R41046, Multifamily and Commercial Mortgages: An Overview of Issues, by N. Eric Weiss.

[2] Terms that are italicized the first time they are used in this report are included in the glossary in the Appendix.

[3] Different types of single-family properties might require different types of mortgages or might influence the type of mortgage that a borrower takes out. For example, mortgages used to purchase condominiums or co-ops might have different requirements than mortgages used to purchase detached single-family homes.

[4] For more information on what closing costs can include, see the Federal Reserve Board, "A Consumer's Guide to Mortgage Settlement Costs," at http://www.federalreserve.gov/ pubs/settlement/default.htm.

[5] The form is made available by the Department of Housing and Urban Development (HUD) and is known as a HUD-1. A sample HUD-1 is available on HUD's website at http://www.hud. gov/offices/adm/hudclips/forms/files/1.pdf. Lenders are also required to provide borrowers with additional disclosures earlier in the mortgage origination process including a good faith estimate (GFE) that provides the borrower with an estimate of anticipated closing costs. For more information on required borrower disclosures, see CRS Report R41980, Revisiting Mortgage Loan Disclosures Under the Consumer Financial Protection Bureau, by Darryl E. Getter and Sean M. Hoskins.

[6] Daniel J. McDonald and Daniel L. Thornton, "A Primer on the Mortgage Market and Mortgage Finance," Federal Reserve Bank of St. Louis, January/February 2008, http://research. stlouisfed.org/publications/review/08/01/ McDonald.pdf. In addition to the four characteristics mentioned above, a mortgage may include other characteristics, such as whether there is a prepayment penalty (a fee that may have to be paid if a borrower attempts to end the mortgage contract before a specified date). However, the four listed characteristics are generally the main focus.

[7] The interest rate is likely to have a ceiling and a floor and only be able to adjust by a fixed amount at a given time. The specifics may vary by individual mortgages. Some mortgages may have an interest rate that is fixed for a given time before becoming adjustable. For example, a 2/28 mortgage has a fixed interest rate for the first two years and an adjustable rate for the existing 28 years.

[8] The $1,264 payment would cover the monthly principal and interest payment on the mortgage. In addition, each month the borrower might also pay property taxes and insurance premiums into her escrow account as part of her monthly payment. An escrow account is an account that a borrower may pay into with part of his monthly payment to ensure the payment of taxes and insurance. The account is a special account that can only be used to make tax and insurance payments on behalf of the borrower.

[9] A borrower could also refinance as a "cash out refinancing." In a cash out refinancing, the borrower refinances the home by taking out a mortgage with a larger principal amount than is needed to extinguish the existing mortgage. The borrower keeps the difference. A borrower will typically need to have built up sufficient equity in the home for cash out refinancing to be approved.

[10] In some cases, it is possible that the borrower could still owe the lender the difference between the sales price of the house and the mortgage amount owed. This will depend on state law and, in states where the borrower can be held responsible for the difference, whether the lender chooses to forgive that amount or not.

[11] To determine the value of the house, the lender may require an appraisal, which is an independent valuation of the home.

[12] In addition to the down payment, the borrower would need to save enough to cover the closing costs of the mortgage. Closing costs are the fees associated with the mortgage settlement process.

[13] For more information on FHA-insured mortgages, see CRS Report RS20530, FHA-Insured Home Loans: An Overview, by Katie Jones.

[14] For more information on VA-guaranteed mortgages, see CRS Report R42504, VA Housing: Guaranteed Loans, Direct Loans, and Specially Adapted Housing Grants, by Libby Perl.

[15] For more information on USDA-guaranteed mortgages, see CRS Report RL31837, An Overview of USDA Rural Development Programs, by Tadlock Cowan.

[18] As with foreclosure, in some states it is possible that the borrower could still owe the lender the difference between the sales price of the house and the mortgage amount owed. See footnote 10.

[19] See CRS Report RS22172, The Conforming Loan Limit, by N. Eric Weiss and Sean M. Hoskins.

[20] Borrowers with jumbo loans can still be considered prime borrowers if they have a good credit history.

[21] One commonly used metric to determine a borrower's classification is the borrower's credit score at the time the loan is originated. There is no single commonly agreed-upon definition, but under one typical definition, borrowers with scores above 660 are considered prime; scores between 620 and 659 are Alt-A; scores below 620 are considered subprime. See Office of the Comptroller of the Currency, OCC Mortgage Metrics Report, at http://www.occ.treas.gov/publications/publications-by-type/other-publications-reports/mortgage-metrics-2012/mortgage-metrics-q3-2012.pdf.

[22] This discussion of risks describes risks to the lender that originates the mortgage, but the discussion is also applicable to any other entity that might purchase the mortgage from the original lender, such as an investor. "The Secondary Market" section of this report describes how mortgages are bought and sold.

[23] Borrowers also prepay the mortgage when they sell the house.

[24] Pooling and servicing agreements (PSAs) are contracts negotiated between the investors and servicers to guide the actions of servicers when borrowers are delinquent on their mortgage payments. PSAs generally instruct the servicer to act in the best interest of the investors. See CRS Report R40210, Preserving Homeownership: Foreclosure Prevention Initiatives, by Katie Jones.

[25] A loan could be sold multiple times before it is eventually securitized, often from a smaller lender to a larger lender that pools the loans.

[26] The tranches could be structured in many different ways. For example, an MBS could be structured as a pass-through security, such that, if an investor purchases 10% of the security, then the investor is entitled to receive 10% of the payments made by borrowers. Alternatively, an MBS could have tiered tranches with the highest tranche entitled to the first stream of payments that borrowers make (and assuming the least amount of risk) and the lowest tranche entitled to the remaining payments (and assuming the most risk).

[27] For more information on servicers' role in mortgage modifications, see CRS Report R40210, Preserving Homeownership: Foreclosure Prevention Initiatives, by Katie Jones.

[28] By law, Ginnie Mae MBS can only contain federally insured mortgages. By law, Fannie Mae and Freddie Mac can only purchase conforming mortgages, and they have not found it profitable to purchase and securitize government-insured mortgages. Because of their GSE

status, Fannie Mae and Freddie Mac have been able to offer better prices in the secondary mortgage market for conforming mortgages. Private-label securitizers have not been able to compete with the GSEs in issuing MBS backed by conforming mortgages.

[29] Congress also established the Federal Home Loan Bank (FHLB) Board and the 12 regional Federal Home Loan Banks in the 1930s. Savings and loans, which were devoted to mortgage lending, were the original members. Initially, Freddie Mac was part of the FHLB System.

[30] Wayne Passmore, Roger Sparks, and Jamie Ingpen, "GSEs, Mortgage Rates, and the Long-Run Effects of Mortgage," December 2001, at http://www.federalreserve.gov /pubs/feds/2001/200126/200126pap.pdf. Although the GSEs may result in lower mortgage interest rates, some of the funding advantage of the GSEs went to investors and company management.

[31] For more information on Fannie Mae's and Freddie Mac's financial status, see CRS Report R42760, Fannie Mae's and Freddie Mac's Financial Status: Frequently Asked Questions, by N. Eric Weiss.

[32] See CRS Report RL34364, Bond Insurers: Issues for the 110th Congress, by Baird Webel and Darryl E. Getter.

[33] Larry Cordell, Yilin Huang, and Meredith Williams, "Collateral Damage: Sizing and Assessing the Subprime CDO Crisis," May 2012 at http://www.philadelphiafed. org/research-and-data/publications/working-papers/2011/wp11- 30.pdf.

[34] The six general parameters include the issuer, maturity, coupon, price, par amount, and settlement date. James Vickery and Joshua Wright, TBA Trading and Liquidity in the Agency MBS Market, Federal Reserve Bank of New York, at http://www.newyorkfed. org/research/epr/2013/1212vick.pdf.

[35] The SIFMA guidelines are called the Uniform Practices for the Clearance and Settlement of Mortgage-Backed Securities and Other Related Securities.

[36] James Vickery and Joshua Wright, TBA Trading and Liquidity in the Agency MBS Market, Federal Reserve Bank of New York, at http://www.newyorkfed.org/ research/ epr/2013/1212vick.pdf.

[37] SIFMA, "TBA Market Fact Sheet," at http://www.sifma.org/issues/item.aspx?id=23775.

In: Housing Finance …
Editor: Sally G. Mitchell

ISBN: 978-1-63482-877-2
© 2015 Nova Science Publishers, Inc.

Chapter 2

TRANSITIONING TO ALTERNATIVE STRUCTURES FOR HOUSING FINANCE*

David Torregrosa

NOTE

Unless otherwise indicated, years referred to in this report are federal fiscal years (which run from October 1 to September 30).

SUMMARY

More than six years after the federal government took control of Fannie Mae and Freddie Mac, policy-makers are weighing a comprehensive overhaul of the mortgage finance system that could shrink or eventually close the two entities and create a system with more private capital. Fannie Mae and Freddie Mac were originally chartered as government-sponsored enterprises (GSEs) to ensure a stable supply of credit for residential mortgages nationwide.[1] They operate in the secondary (or resale) market where they buy mortgages from the financial institutions that make the loans (thus ensuring that those institutions have a source of funds to originate new mortgages). Fannie Mae and Freddie

* This is an edited, reformatted and augmented version of a report issued by the Congressional Budget Office, December 2014.

Mac then pool those loans to create mortgage-backed securities (MBSs), which they guarantee against defaults on principal and interest payments by borrowers and sell to investors.

Through its financial commitment to the two GSEs and its other mortgage programs, the federal government now directly or indirectly insures over 70 percent of all new residential mortgages. Loans guaranteed by Fannie Mae and Freddie Mac account for over two-thirds of those mortgages (about 50 percent of the total amount of mortgages), and loans insured by the Federal Housing Administration (FHA) make up most of the remaining federal share. Such government dominance was not always the case—in the 20 years before the financial crisis that began in 2007, roughly half of all mortgages were financed without backing from the federal government or either of the GSEs.

As the effects of the financial crisis have receded and as the housing market has recovered, policymakers have taken some initial steps toward returning to a secondary mortgage market with more private-sector involvement. Those steps include raising the fees that Fannie Mae and Freddie Mac charge for their guarantees to levels that private firms may be better able to compete with. The Congressional Budget Office (CBO) expects that the steps already taken, together with pending changes to financial regulations, will reduce the two GSEs' share of the mortgage market over the next 10 years.

This report examines various mechanisms that policy-makers could use to attract more private capital to the secondary mortgage market. The report also addresses how those mechanisms could be combined in different ways to help the market make the transition to a new structure during the coming decade. CBO analyzed transition paths to four alternative structures that involve choices about whether the government would continue to guarantee payment on mortgages and MBSs and, if so, what form and prices those guarantees would have.[2] Under those different structures, the government's activities would range from providing full or partial guarantees for a large share of the mortgage market to playing a minimal role in a largely private market (except perhaps during a financial crisis). Any transition to a new type of secondary market would also require decisions about what to do with the existing operations, guarantee obligations, and investment holdings of Fannie Mae and Freddie Mac.

CBO's analysis has three key findings:

- A transition to a new structure for housing finance that emphasized private capital could reduce costs and risks to taxpayers. One drawback to such a transition is that mortgages could become somewhat less available and more expensive to borrowers. Thus, over the longer term, it could also result in a modest shift of the economy's resources away from housing toward other activities.

- Although the transition to a new structure could significantly decrease the number of borrowers who received mortgages backed by Fannie Mae or Freddie Mac, additional private capital would replace most of the lost funding. Borrowers would probably not face significant increases in interest rates because the two GSEs' current pricing is not too far below market pricing. Consequently, a gradual transition would probably exert only modest downward pressure on house prices.
- Because policymakers have already raised the guarantee fees charged by Fannie Mae and Freddie Mac close to those that CBO estimates would be charged by private insurers, the budgetary costs of the two GSEs' activities over the next 10 years are expected to be small. As a result, the budgetary savings would also be small under any of the transition paths to a more private system that CBO considered. Thus, the choice between the different market structures probably rests primarily on considerations other than budgetary costs. (Those findings depend on the accounting framework that CBO uses for Fannie Mae and Freddie Mac, as described below.)

CBO's projections of budgetary costs and the size of the federal role in the mortgage market involve considerable uncertainty. In particular, because the market for mortgages is now dominated by large government-backed entities, the price that private investors would charge to bear the risks of mortgage guarantees and how that price might evolve over time are highly uncertain. CBO based its projections on its assessment of the middle of the distribution of estimates of that price.

What Options Would Attract More Private Capital?

CBO expects that the role of Fannie Mae and Freddie Mac in the secondary mortgage market will shrink over the next decade under current policy. If policymakers wanted to reduce that role further and lessen the advantages given to the two GSEs, they could use various mechanisms:

- Raise guarantee fees on new mortgages further to bring the two GSEs' pricing closer to pricing in the private market.[†] Even small increases in those fees would nearly eliminate budgetary costs for Fannie Mae and Freddie Mac (using the accounting framework described below) and allow private firms to capture some of the GSEs' current business.
- Change the limits on the maximum size of mortgages that Fannie Mae and Freddie Mac are allowed to guarantee. The limit is currently $625,500 in areas with high housing costs and $417,000 in the rest of the country, although the average size of new mortgages guaranteed by the two GSEs is only about $200,000 in 2014.
- Share the credit risk of mortgages (the risk of loss when a borrower defaults) with private investors— for example, offer compensation to induce private investors to assume responsibility for the initial losses on GSE-guaranteed loans.
- Auction off a limited number of new guarantees by Fannie Mae and Freddie Mac to the highest bidders rather than requiring the GSEs to continue to guarantee all eligible mortgages submitted by lenders for preset fees, thus reducing the size of the two GSEs' guarantee business. Auctions would determine the market prices of those guarantees and allocate them to the lenders who most valued them.

How those mechanisms were used, whether alone or in combination, would depend on which new structure for the secondary mortgage market policymakers wanted to encourage. Changes in the GSEs' guarantee fees and loan limits could be useful for many types of restructuring, whereas risk sharing and auctions would be more appropriate for a transition to a smaller, but continuing, federal presence in the market. (The Federal Housing Finance Agency, which regulates the GSEs, currently has the authority to employ any of those mechanisms, although CBO's budget projections for Fannie Mae and Freddie Mac are based on the assumptions that their present fee levels and loan limits will continue and that risk sharing with private investors will remain limited.)

[†] Sentence corrected on December 30, 2014.

What Structures for the Secondary Market Did CBO Consider, and What Would a Transition to Them Involve?

For this analysis, CBO packaged the aforementioned policy mechanisms into illustrative transition paths that, between 2015 and 2024, would move the secondary mortgage market from dominance by two large government-sponsored enterprises to one of four alternative structures (see Summary Table 1):

- A market with a single, fully federal agency that would carry out the two GSEs' main function of buying eligible mortgages and turning them into securities that are guaranteed against losses from default on the underlying mortgages. The transition to such an agency would require little or no change to the structure of the GSEs' guarantees, the fees charged for them, or the GSEs' loan limits because no significant amounts of new private capital would be required beyond those that are expected to be invested under current policy. By the end of the transition period, the federal agency would have a smaller share of the market than Fannie Mae and Freddie Mac have today.
- A hybrid public-private market with federal guarantees against catastrophic losses. Under that structure, the government and private investors would share credit losses on eligible MBSs, with federal guarantees covering catastrophic risks (those associated with severe downturns in the housing market) for a significant share of mortgages. As a result, taxpayers would bear most of the losses during a crisis, but private investors would bear most of the losses in other periods. The main policy mechanism used to transition to that structure would be sharing credit risk with private investors.
- A market with the federal government as "guarantor of last resort," in which private companies would guarantee most new mortgages in normal times, but the government would fully guarantee most new mortgages during financial crises. (In normal times, the government would guarantee a small sample of mortgages of all sizes to ensure that it is capable of doing so in times of crisis.) The major policy actions taken to establish the new structure would be auctioning off the GSEs' new guarantees and raising their loan limits.
- A largely private market with no explicit federal guarantees of MBSs (other than those provided by the Government National Mortgage Association, which securitizes and guarantees mortgages insured by

other federal agencies, such as FHA and the Department of Veterans Affairs). That structure would minimize the explicit credit risk borne by taxpayers. The main policy changes made during the transition would be raising guarantee fees and lowering loan limits until the GSEs no longer guaranteed new mortgages.

Those alternative market structures share some common features (although those features might be altered through policy changes that lie beyond the scope of this report). The government would guarantee only mortgages that met certain eligibility criteria, and private financial institutions would provide most other mortgages. FHA would continue to provide assistance to low-income homebuyers. Under all of the structures, the portfolios of mortgages that Fannie Mae and Freddie Mac hold as investments would be reduced. Depending on the new structure, the two GSEs could be incorporated into a single federal agency, liquidated (with their operating systems sold to private investors), or privatized. Any transition would involve legal and regulatory issues that would necessarily take some time to resolve, which is why CBO examined transitions that would take place over a 10-year period.

How Would the Transition to Those Structures Affect Borrowers, the Housing Market, and the Federal Budget?

If policymakers reduced the role of Fannie Mae and Freddie Mac, borrowers would probably face somewhat higher interest rates on mortgages, and house prices would probably decline modestly (see Summary Table 2). The increases in interest rates that borrowers faced, however, would probably be smaller than the fluctuations in market interest rates that occur during a typical year. Borrowers would most likely continue to have access to 30-year fixed rate mortgages as long as the market for converting mortgages into MBSs was large and the securities were easily traded, whether or not that market had government backing. Lending standards would most likely be higher on privately backed mortgages, and during a financial crisis, the availability of those private loans could be sharply disrupted, causing their costs to rise significantly.

Summary Table 1. Key Features of CBO's Illustrative Transition Paths to New Structures for the Secondary Mortgage Market

	Current Policy (GSEs remain in conservatorship)	Transition to a Market With a Single, Fully Federal Agency	Transition to a Hybrid Public-Private Market	Transition to a Market With the Government as Guarantor of Last Resort	Transition to a Largely Private Secondary Market
Key Policy Changes	Not applicable	Establish new federal agency	Increase sharing of credit risk	Hold auctions and aise loan limits	Raise fees and reduce loan limits
GSEs' Guarantee Feesa	Current fee schedule, including 10 basis-point drop in 2022, remains (Fees averaged 55 basis points in January 2014)	No changes	Small increasesb	Fees set by auction; would probably rise toward fair-value level	Large initial increase followed by smaller increases, for a total rise of 50 basis points by 2022b
GSEs' Loan Limits[c]	$625,500 in high-cost areas, $417,000 elsewhere	Reduced to $417,000 in all areas	Reduced to $417,000 in all areas	Raised to $729,750 in all areas	Gradually reduced to zero
Sharing of Credit Riskd	Private mortgage insurance required for borrowers with less than 20 percent down payment	No changes	Investors take first losses from default; GSEs guarantee against catastrophic losses	No changes	No changes

Summary Table 1. (Continued)

	Current Policy (GSEs remain in conservatorship)	Transition to a Market With a Single, Fully Federal Agency	Transition to a Hybrid Public-Private Market	Transition to a Market With the Government as Guarantor of Last Resort	Transition to a Largely Private Secondary Market
Auctions of New GSE Guarantees	None	None	None	Amount of new GSE guarantees auctioned off gradually reduced until GSEs cover only a small share of the market	None

Source: Congressional Budget Office.

Notes: A basis point is 0.01 percentage point.

GSEs = government-sponsored enterprises (specifically, Fannie Mae and Freddie Mac).

[a] In exchange for guaranteeing the timely payment of interest and principal on a mortgage, the GSEs receive fees from the lender (or the company servicing the lender's loans).

[b] In this transition path, the 10 basis-point increase in the GSEs' guarantee fees enacted in the Temporary Payroll Tax Cut Continuation Act of 2011, which is due to expire on October 1, 2021, is assumed to be extended permanently.

[c] Lawmakers have limited the size of mortgages that are eligible to be included in pools of loans guaranteed by the GSEs.

[d] In this case, sharing credit risk means that private parties absorb some amount of losses from loan defaults before the GSEs are required to do so.

Summary Table 2. Probable Effects of CBO's Illustrative Transition Paths on Subsidy Costs, Loan Guarantees, and the Mortgage and Housing Markets

	Transition to a Market With a Single, Fully Federal Agency	Transition to a Hybrid Public-Private Market	Transition to a Market With the Government as Guarantor of Last Resort	Transition to a Largely Private Secondary Market
Federal Subsidy Costs for the GSEs	Slight increases throughout the transition	Reduced to nearly zero by the end of the transition	Large declines throughout the transition	Reduced to zero by the end of the transition
Volume of New Loan Guarantees by the GSEs	Small declines throughout the transition	Moderate declines throughout the transition	Large decline by the end of the transition	Reduced to zero by the end of the transition
Availability of Credit During a Financial Crisis	Not affected	Less available	Not affected	Less available
Availability of 30-Year Fixed Rate Mortgages	Not affected	Not affected	Probably disrupted when the securitization market is frozen	Probably disrupted when the securitization market is frozen
Interest Rates for Most Borrowers of GSE-Backed Mortgages	Not affected (Slight increases throughout the transition on loans without GSE backing)	Small increases throughout the transition	Small increases throughout the transition (Larger increases on loans without GSE backing)	Moderate increases by the end of the transition (Larger increases throughout the transition on loans without GSE backing)
House Prices	Not noticeably affected	Slightly lower throughout the transition	Slightly lower by the end of the transition	Slightly lower by the end of the transition

Summary Table 2. (Continued)

	Transition to a Market With a Single, Fully Federal Agency	Transition to a Hybrid Public-Private Market	Transition to a Market With the Government as Guarantor of Last Resort	Transition to a Largely Private Secondary Market
Investment in Housing	Current overallocation of capital toward housing would continue	Allocation of capital toward housing would be reduced	Allocation of capital toward housing would be reduced	Allocation of capital toward housing would be reduced
Volume of Loans Insured by FHA	Small increases throughout the transition	Moderate increases throughout the transition	Moderate increases throughout the transition	Large increases by the end of the transition
Other Effects	Federal government would maintain control of a large segment of the capital market	GSEs' credit losses from defaults would drop significantly	Market mechanisms would ensure that guarantee fees reflect risk more fully	Financial institutions would have the strongest incentive to be prudent in their lending and securitizing

Source: Congressional Budget Office.

Notes: These effects are relative to CBO's projections of outcomes during the 2015–2024 period under current policy.

GSEs = government-sponsored enterprises (specifically, Fannie Mae and Freddie Mac); FHA = Federal Housing Administration.

Under current policy, CBO expects that Fannie Mae and Freddie Mac will guarantee, on average, about $1 trillion of new mortgages per year over the next decade but that their overall share of the mortgage market will decline from over 50 percent now to about 40 percent by 2024. CBO projects that the present value of the government's total income and payments over the life of those mortgages will translate to costs of about $19 billion for taxpayers over that period (estimated on a fair-value basis, as described below). Those budgetary costs would be significantly reduced in a transition to any of the market structures that CBO analyzed except in the transition to a market with a single, fully federal agency. (In that transition, costs over the next 10 years would rise slightly.)

Under all of the illustrative transition paths, some borrowers who would have had GSE-backed mortgages under current policy would shift to FHA-insured loans rather than to privately backed loans. CBO estimates that the increase in the volume of mortgages for single-family homes guaranteed by FHA would range from relatively small—in the transition to a market with a single, fully federal agency—to significant—in the transition to a largely private market. Because the two GSEs and FHA are accounted for differently in CBO's estimates of the federal budget (as described below), the shift in guarantees from Fannie Mae and Freddie Mac to FHA would have the effect of increasing the budgetary savings projected for the transition paths, even though the risk borne by taxpayers would be little changed.

How Does CBO Account for Fannie Mae, Freddie Mac, and FHA in Its Budget Estimates?

The estimates of budgetary costs in this report depend on the accounting treatment that CBO uses for the two GSEs and FHA. CBO accounts for the costs of Fannie Mae's and Freddie Mac's activities on a fair-value basis, in which estimated costs represent an approximation of the price that the federal government would need to pay a private insurer to make loan guarantees on the same terms as the GSEs. Because those fair-value estimates incorporate a charge for market risk—the additional compensation that private investors demand to invest in risky assets such as mortgages—they provide a more comprehensive measure of the costs of guarantees than do projections of the net cash costs associated with guarantees.

That choice of accounting method has two consequences for CBO's analysis:

- Transactions that occurred at market prices in liquid and orderly markets would have no fair-value costs. Thus, regardless of which structure for the secondary market was ultimately adopted, the cost or savings to the government from transferring the GSEs' existing mortgage assets or guarantee obligations to private investors would probably be small under fair-value accounting. If, instead, CBO accounted for the GSEs' activities on a cash basis, as the Administration does, those transactions would result in costs for the government because the GSEs would lose future streams of income, which would include at least some compensation for market risk.
- The fair-value approach would probably show small savings from a transition that reduced the volume of new guarantees by Fannie Mae and Freddie Mac and increased the role of the private sector in the secondary mortgage market. If, instead, CBO accounted for the GSEs' activities on a cash basis, that same transition would probably result in large estimated costs to the government. Specifically, the GSEs' current activities are expected to produce cash savings for the government because Fannie Mae and Freddie Mac charge enough for their loan guarantees to more than cover the projected losses on of those guarantees (though not enough to cover the risks that a competitive private insurance company would factor in when charging for the same guarantees).[3]

In contrast to CBO's treatment of Fannie Mae and Freddie Mac, guarantees by FHA, like the activities of most other federal credit programs, are accounted for in the budget using the procedures specified in the Federal Credit Reform Act of 1990. Unlike the fair-value approach, those procedures do not incorporate market risk. As a result of those differences in accounting, additional savings would be reported in the budget as some borrowers shifted from GSE financing to FHA guarantees.

Section 1. The Secondary Mortgage Market under Current Policy

In September 2008, the federal government put Fannie Mae and Freddie Mac, the two giants of the mortgage finance system, into conservatorship—a legal process that allows the government to control the institutions and their business practices and to set their strategic goals. That move came as falling home prices and rising delinquencies on mortgages threatened the solvency of the two institutions and hampered their ability to facilitate the flow of credit to mortgage borrowers. The government pledged hundreds of billions of dollars to shore up Fannie Mae and Freddie Mac in exchange for almost complete ownership—in effect, transforming them into federal entities and reinforcing their already dominant position in the secondary (or resale) market for residential mortgages. The government's expanded role has increased the availability of mortgage credit and has helped stabilize the housing market and the economy. However, mortgage credit carries with it the risk of financial losses if borrowers default—known as mortgage credit risk—and the government's expanded role has transferred that risk to taxpayers.

In the secondary market, lenders that originate mortgages (such as banks and mortgage companies) generally obtain funds to make more loans by selling their mortgages to Fannie Mae, Freddie Mac, and other buyers (including banks and insurance companies). Selling loans to Fannie Mae and Freddie Mac is often the cheapest source of funding, especially for a 30-year fixed rate mortgage. Those two institutions and other buyers generally package such loans into mortgage-backed securities (MBSs), which they sell to investors along with a guarantee of payment on the underlying mortgages—a process known as securitization.[1] In essence, an MBS represents a claim on the cash flows from the pool of mortgages included in the security.

Since the financial crisis that began in 2007, the willingness of private investors and firms to assume responsibility for mortgage credit risk has declined sharply. As a result, the secondary mortgage market is now almost entirely federal. The Congressional Budget Office (CBO) expects the private sector's role in that market to increase over time—and the role of Fannie Mae and Freddie Mac to diminish—as the adverse effects of the financial crisis wane and the housing market recovers. Banks, thrift institutions (such as savings and loans), and mortgage brokers still rely on securitization in the secondary market to supply funding for most of the mortgages they originate. Whether that reliance will continue or other low-cost funding alternatives will emerge depends on a number of changes to federal financial regulations that are now pending, as well as on many other factors. However, if banks have few options other than to hold more mortgages on their balance sheets (whether they originated those loans or purchased them from other lenders in the secondary market), the private sector will probably play a smaller than expected role in backing mortgage credit risk.

The Federal Government's Role in the Mortgage Market

In 2013, the government backed about 80 percent of the $1.9 trillion in new residential mortgages. About $1.2 trillion of those mortgages were guaranteed by Fannie Mae and Freddie Mac. Many of the rest were insured by the Federal Housing Administration (FHA), which has since 2008 ramped up its insurance of loans for borrowers who lack the savings, credit history, or income to qualify for mortgages guaranteed by Fannie Mae and Freddie Mac. The government's share of the market fell to just over 70 percent in the first six months of 2014, as private companies played a bigger role.

Activities of Fannie Mae and Freddie Mac

More than four decades ago, the Congress chartered Fannie Mae and Freddie Mac as government-sponsored enterprises (GSEs)—private corporations with the public mission of promoting access to mortgage credit by increasing the liquidity of mortgage investments (that is, ensuring that mortgages can be readily bought and sold). Those GSEs are also required to promote affordable housing for low- and moderate-income families.[2] (Although Fannie Mae and Freddie Mac are now owned and run by the federal government, CBO still refers to them as GSEs for simplicity and because they differ from fully federal agencies in some significant legal and institutional ways.)

To carry out their missions, the two GSEs buy certain home loans from lenders and package them into MBSs, which are sold to investors. (Fannie Mae and Freddie Mac are forbidden by their charters from originating mortgages themselves.) In exchange for the GSEs' guarantee of timely payment of interest and principal on those loans, the lenders (or companies servicing their loans) pay the GSEs a monthly fee, which is based mainly on the type of loan involved, as well as an up-front fee, which is based on the riskiness of the loan. Those fees are effectively paid by mortgage borrowers—either up front when they take out a loan or as part of their monthly interest payments. Besides selling MBSs, Fannie Mae and Freddie Mac also buy some MBSs to hold in their portfolios as investments; they fund those purchases by issuing debt securities.

To control their exposure to the risk of loss from defaults, the two GSEs set and enforce standards for the characteristics of the loans they purchase, such as borrowers' creditworthiness, the size of down payments, and, on some loans, requirements for private mortgage insurance. The GSEs require lenders to make "representations and warranties" that their underwriting and documentation meet those contractual standards. In the past several years, Fannie Mae and Freddie Mac have received large payments from lenders in settlements related to alleged breaches of the standards. (Concern about such settlements has caused lenders to tighten their lending standards, making it harder for some borrowers to obtain mortgages.)[3]

The size of the mortgages that Fannie Mae and Freddie Mac can purchase is limited by statute. For loans on single-family homes, that limit is currently $625,500 in areas with high housing costs (down from $729,750 during the financial crisis) and $417,000 in other areas. Mortgages that are under those limits and that meet the GSEs' other standards are known as conforming loans.

Providing credit guarantees to investors who buy mortgage-backed securities, which makes those securities safer for investors, is the primary way that Fannie Mae and Freddie Mac enhance liquidity and reduce the probability and severity of disruptions in the financing of mortgages. The GSEs also promote liquidity by standardizing the securitization process. Securities, whether they are federally backed or privately issued, are easier to trade if they are issued in large volumes and are relatively homogeneous and interchangeable. Such securities require less specialized knowledge on the part of investors and thus appeal to a broader base of investors. The guarantees and standardization reduce interest rates on mortgages.

Some of the benefits that the two GSEs provide are the result of federal subsidies. Fannie Mae and Freddie Mac are now explicitly backed by the federal government, which increases the value of their guarantees to investors. But even before conservatorship, investors generally assumed that Fannie Mae's and Freddie Mac's MBSs carried an implicit federal guarantee. (That assumption was proved correct when the federal government took over the two GSEs rather than let them become insolvent.) Under normal market conditions, using federal guarantees to support liquidity in the secondary mortgage market tends to reduce interest rates only slightly for most mortgage borrowers. Such government support had the greatest impact on the availability and price of mortgages during the financial crisis and its aftermath. That support, although risky to taxpayers, reduced the extent to which the crisis spilled over to the market for new-home construction and helped protect the broader economy.

In periods of extreme financial distress, even a federal guarantee may not be enough to ensure a stable source of low-cost funding for the secondary market. At such times, the government can also support liquidity by standing ready to buy large amounts of MBSs—as the Federal Reserve and, to a much smaller extent, the Treasury did in response to the most recent crisis.[4] From

September 2012 to December 2013, the Federal Reserve purchased about $40 billion of mortgage-backed securities each month, most of them issued by Fannie Mae and Freddie Mac. The amount of those purchases steadily declined from January 2014 to October 2014, when the Federal Reserve announced that it would stop purchasing MBSs at the end of the month. As of October 30, 2014, the Federal Reserve held $1.7 trillion of mortgage-backed securities.

Conservatorship

In the summer of 2008, the size of Fannie Mae's and Freddie Mac's losses on their outstanding guarantees and investment portfolios impaired their ability to buy mortgages and to continue making payments on their obligations. As a result, on September 6 of that year, the Secretary of the Treasury and the director of the Federal Housing Finance Agency (FHFA) placed the two GSEs in conservatorship, exercising their authority under the Housing and Economic Recovery Act (enacted in July 2008). That law allows the Treasury to provide funds to the GSEs to keep their net worth from falling below zero, effectively insuring holders of their debt securities and MBSs against losses. In return for that support, which takes the form of purchases of the GSEs' preferred stock, the Treasury receives quarterly payments from Fannie Mae and Freddie Mac and rights to nearly 80 percent ownership of their common stock.

In 2012, the Treasury and the two GSEs revised their agreements: Rather than pay a fixed dividend on the Treasury's preferred shares, Fannie Mae and Freddie Mac began in 2013 to return almost all of their profits to the Treasury. However, those payments do not reduce the amount of preferred stock held by the Treasury, and the GSEs are prohibited from buying back that stock under their agreements with the Treasury and FHFA. Thus, the terms of the agreements and the conservatorship ensure that the federal government effectively retains complete ownership and control of Fannie Mae and Freddie Mac.

FHFA, which is responsible for regulating the safety and soundness of the two GSEs, acts as conservator. It oversees the GSEs' operations and sets goals for their performance. In doing so, FHFA pursues several aims: minimizing losses on behalf of taxpayers, supporting a stable and liquid mortgage market, maximizing assistance to homeowners, and minimizing foreclosures. To help struggling borrowers, FHFA has implemented loan modification programs (which generally reduce the interest rates on mortgages rather than the principal) and has streamlined refinancing programs.[5] In addition, the agency has directed the GSEs to limit their portfolio holdings and to experiment with bulk sales of real estate acquired through foreclosures. It has also replaced senior managers at Fannie Mae and Freddie Mac and limited executive compensation.

The two GSEs' share of the housing finance market has expanded since conservatorship began. As of June 30, 2014, Fannie Mae and Freddie Mac owned or guaranteed roughly half of the nearly $10 trillion in outstanding single-family residential mortgages in the United States; they backed about 60 percent of the estimated $1.9 trillion in new mortgages in 2013 and about 50 percent of the mortgages originated in the first half of 2014, whereas in 2006 they backed less than 30 percent of new mortgages (see Figure 1-1).[6] In response to past losses, the GSEs have tightened their credit standards.

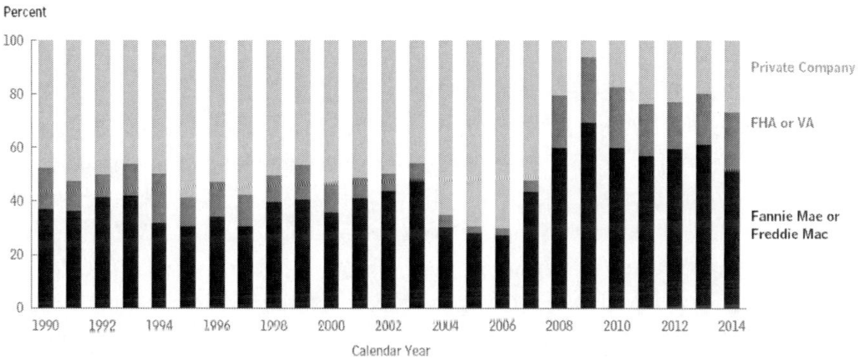

Source: Congressional Budget Office based on data from *Inside Mortgage Finance*.

Notes: The market shares shown here represent the distribution of all single-family residential mortgages (including home-equity loans) originated in a given year, by the entities that guarantee or (in the case of unguaranteed mortgages) hold them. "Single-family" mortgages are loans for units that house one to four families.

Data for 2014 are through June 30, 2014.

FHA = Federal Housing Administration; VA = Department of Veterans Affairs.

Figure 1-1. Shares of the Market for New Single-Family Residential Mortgages, by Guarantor or Holder.

In the face of the two GSEs' expanding market share, FHFA and lawmakers have begun taking actions to encourage greater involvement by the private sector in the housing finance market. Those actions include reducing the size limit for the mortgages that the GSEs are allowed to purchase in high-cost areas (from $729,750 to $625,500) and raising the GSEs' guarantee fees (which are still lower than those that would be charged by private companies).[7] Lawmakers increased Fannie Mae's and Freddie Mac's guarantee fees by 10 basis points (0.1 percentage point) through September 30, 2021, in the Temporary Payroll Tax Cut Continuation Act of 2011. FHFA implemented an additional fee increase of 10 basis points in late 2012 and has expanded the use of up-front fees (called loan-level price adjustments, delivery fees, and adverse market charges) to better align the pricing of MBS guarantees with the riskiness of the underlying mortgages. As a result, in January 2014, the GSEs' average guarantee fee for new loans (including both up-front and ongoing fees) was about 55 basis points of a loan's principal, whereas before the financial crisis, it was about 20 basis points.

Another action that could expand private-sector involvement is the joint venture between Fannie Mae and Freddie Mac, announced in March 2013, to create and operate a common infrastructure for securitizing mortgages. That infrastructure might eventually be used by private issuers of MBSs as well.[8]

Activities of the Federal Housing Administration

The Federal Housing Administration—which provides insurance against default to lenders for certain mortgages—has also played a much larger role since the financial crisis, as have smaller programs for federally insured mortgages, such as those run by the Department of Veterans Affairs and the Rural Housing Service. Almost all of the loans insured by those federal agencies are securitized and fully guaranteed by the Government National Mortgage Association (Ginnie Mae), whose activities in the secondary mortgage market have increased in recent years as well.

Because FHA insures loans with down payments as low as 3.5 percent, it is now the primary source of financing for first-time homebuyers. The share of new mortgages that FHA insures each year, which averaged just 4 percent between 2000 and 2007, jumped to an average of 15 percent from 2008 to 2011 and peaked at 18 percent in 2009. In 2013, FHA guaranteed about 12 percent (over $200 billion) of new mortgages.

After experiencing high default rates on loans issued between 2005 and 2007, before the worst of the financial crisis began, FHA raised premiums for its mortgage insurance and tightened its underwriting standards starting in 2008. Currently, the majority of borrowers who take out 30-year fixed rate mortgages and make down payments of less than 5 percent pay annual insurance premiums of 135 basis points, plus an up-front fee of 175 basis points. Those FHA fees are considerably higher than the fees charged by Fannie Mae and Freddie Mac because of the greater risk associated with FHA loans.

Developments in the Private Market

The federal government's role in the mortgage market expanded in recent years because private firms and investors sharply reduced their willingness to issue or hold mortgages without a federal guarantee. Historically, private-sector participants in the secondary market supplied funding for mortgages by issuing their own mortgage-backed securities (referred to as private-label MBSs). Between 2009 and 2011, however, that activity virtually ceased. Although it has picked up since then, the rate of securitization by private issuers remains very low. Consequently, banks have recently been holding most of the newly originated mortgages that they do not sell to the GSEs or Ginnie Mae on their balance sheets and bearing the credit risk, which is a departure from past practice. (For the past 25 years, banks had been shifting their mortgage-related portfolios toward MBSs and away from whole, rather than securitized, loans. That shift occurred in part because banks are required to hold more capital to absorb potential losses on whole mortgages than on MBSs.)

Since the financial crisis, mortgage originators have tightened their lending standards, even for loans eligible to be guaranteed by Fannie Mae or Freddie Mac. (Because of the representations and warranties that an originator must make to the two GSEs, selling loans to those institutions does not completely eliminate the originator's credit risk.) One reason for the tightening was that the probability of default increased as people's employment prospects became more uncertain and house prices declined.[9] As a result of the changes, the credit score and down payment requirements for borrowers trying to qualify for a conforming mortgage are higher than they were before the crisis, and borrowers must now fully document their income. Recently, however, a modest easing of lending standards for prime residential loans— those that go to borrowers with good credit and low debtto-income ratios—was reported by lenders in a survey conducted by the Federal Reserve.[10]

Another important recent development in the private mortgage market is an apparent reduction in the compensation that investors require to assume the credit risk on privately backed mortgages. That reduction is evidenced by a decrease in the extent to which interest rates on jumbo mortgages (those too large to qualify for a GSE guarantee) exceed interest rates on conforming mortgages. That interest rate differential is a rough indicator of how much value investors place on the GSEs' federal backing.[11] The average spread between those rates was more than 150 basis points at the height of the financial crisis, but it ranged between 10 basis points and 55 basis points in calendar year 2013 and generally remained under 10 basis points in the first 11 months of 2014 (see Figure 1-2). Some of the decline in that spread since the financial crisis resulted from policymakers' raising the GSEs' guarantee fees, but most of the decrease is attributable to private investors' willingness to accept lower compensation for holding mortgage risk. The narrowing of the spread between those interest rates has encouraged more originations of jumbo loans.

Source: Congressional Budget Office based on data from Bloomberg and Bankrate.com.

Notes: Conforming mortgages are ones whose size and terms make them eligible to be guaranteed by Fannie Mae and Freddie Mac. Jumbo mortgages are ones whose size exceeds the limit for conforming mortgages.

A basis point is 0.01 percentage point.

Data are weekly and are plotted through December 3, 2014.

Figure 1-2. Interest Rates on Mortgages With and Without Guarantees by Fannie Mae or Freddie Mac.

Budgetary Treatment of Fannie Mae and Freddie Mac

Since the two GSEs were taken into conservatorship, CBO has treated Fannie Mae and Freddie Mac as government entities for its projections of the federal budget. In projecting the budgetary costs of the entities' new loan guarantees, CBO uses an accrual approach in which the net cost of a guarantee is the present value, as of the date the obligation is incurred, of the expected stream of income and payments over the years from that guarantee. CBO constructs that present value using an interest rate that reflects the price that would be charged by private market participants for taking that risk; those "fair-value" estimates approximate the fair market price that a private guarantor would charge the government to provide the same guarantees. That budgetary treatment differs from the one used by the Administration, which focuses on Fannie Mae's and Freddie Mac's annual cash transactions with the Treasury rather than on the full cost of their loan guarantees.

Measured on a fair-value basis, Fannie Mae's and Freddie Mac's activities are being subsidized by the federal government, because the fees that the institutions charge for their guarantees are lower than what CBO estimates competitive firms would charge—and thus are lower than the estimated costs of those guarantees. In its April 2014 baseline budget projections, CBO estimated that federal subsidies on the new loan guarantees that Fannie Mae and Freddie Mac are expected to make in fiscal year 2015 will amount to $4 billion over the lifetime of those loans and that federal subsidies on the new guarantees made between 2015 and 2024 will total $19 billion.[12] Those lifetime subsidy costs are reported in CBO's budget projections as a single lump-sum outlay in the year in which the guarantees are expected to be made.

As discussed in Section 4, CBO's projections also include the purchases and sales of securities in the GSEs' investment portfolio. As long as those transactions occur at market prices, they will not result in any budgetary gains or losses when measured on a fair-value basis.

What CBO's Fair-Value Estimates Cover

CBO's fair-value estimates of federal subsidies for Fannie Mae and Freddie Mac account for all of the expected cash flows associated with the two GSEs' loan guarantees, including the fees paid by borrowers and the costs incurred by the GSEs when a borrower defaults. Thus, the subsidy estimates are accrual accounting measures (as opposed to cash accounting measures) of the expected lifetime cost of new loan guarantees as of the year in which a loan is disbursed.

The fair-value approach also accounts for market risk— the type of financial risk that investors cannot avoid by diversifying their portfolios. Market risk results from actual or expected changes in overall economic conditions. In practice, the cost of market risk is incorporated by choosing an appropriate interest rate (called a discount rate) to convert the stream of future income and payments into a single present value. For example, the discount rate used by CBO to compute the present value of the cash flows from a mortgage is the rate of return that a well-diversified investor buying a mortgage-backed security in a competitive market would expect to earn while holding the security. As compensation for market risk, investors expect to earn a higher rate of return (even after accounting for expected losses) than they would require to hold an investment without that risk (such as a Treasury security, which most investors consider to have very little market risk). The additional compensation that investors demand for bearing market risk is known as a risk premium.

The federal government is exposed to market risk on the GSEs' guarantees because when the economy is weak, borrowers default on their mortgages more frequently, and the amounts recovered after defaults are lower.[13] When Fannie Mae or Freddie Mac guarantees a mortgage, the market risk associated with that obligation is effectively passed on to taxpayers—who, as investors, would view that risk as having a cost. CBO's budget estimates for the two GSEs are quite sensitive to assumptions about the market risk of the mortgage guarantees, which may be higher or lower than CBO anticipates.

A loan guarantee will have a fair-value subsidy cost if it is priced below what a private firm would charge in a competitive, liquid market (or, equivalently, if it is expected to earn a lower rate of return than other investments with comparable risk). Consequently, if Fannie Mae or Freddie Mac charged 55 basis points a year to guarantee loans but a private company would demand about 65 basis points in compensation to assume the same obligations, the federal subsidy (the missing fees) would be about 10 basis points a year. In practice, CBO's fair-value estimates make some adjustments for differences in liquidity between the markets for GSE and private-sector loan guarantees. The current structure of the secondary mortgage market favors Fannie Mae and Freddie Mac and reduces liquidity for privately backed loans. In addition, the fee that the market would charge for GSE guarantees cannot be directly observed (although some information can be gleaned from Fannie Mae's and Freddie Mac's risk-sharing transactions), so CBO must infer it from other sources. The limited role that the private sector is currently playing in the secondary market also adds to the uncertainty surrounding fair-value estimates.

Instead of a fair-value approach, most federal programs that make loans or loan guarantees are accounted for using procedures specified under the Federal Credit Reform Act of 1990 (FCRA). Although those procedures require that subsidy costs be estimated on a present-value basis, they specify that expected cash flows must be discounted using interest rates on Treasury securities with similar maturities rather than rates of return on riskier assets. The subsidy costs estimated for the two GSEs would be significantly lower under those procedures than under fair-value accounting and would generally appear as savings.[14]

Differences between CBO's and the Administration's Budgetary Treatment of the GSEs

In contrast to CBO's budgetary treatment, the Administration treats Fannie Mae and Freddie Mac as separate from the federal government and reports only their cash transactions with the Treasury. Those transactions consist of payments that the government makes to the two GSEs when it buys their preferred stock and, in the opposite direction, amounts that the GSEs pay to the government.

As of the end of September 2014, the Treasury has purchased $187 billion of senior preferred stock from Fannie Mae and Freddie Mac, and the two GSEs have paid $219 billion to the Treasury under the terms of their agreements with the government.[15] Most of those payments came from the $130 billion in net income that Fannie Mae and Freddie Mac together earned in 2013. (Those earnings were boosted by one-time accounting changes—the revaluation of the GSEs' deferred tax assets, which resulted in additional payments of $75 billion in 2013—and by $8 billion in legal settlements with large banks.) In its budget for fiscal year 2015, the Administration projected that the two institutions would make payments to the government totaling $181.5 billion between January 2014 and September 2024. (Those payments exclude sums that the Treasury collects from the two GSEs from the 10 basis-point increase in guarantee fees enacted in the Temporary Payroll Tax Cut Continuation Act. Those sums totaled about $2 billion in 2014.)

Differences between CBO's and the Administration's budget estimates for Fannie Mae and Freddie Mac do not reflect diverging expectations about the future profitability of those institutions. CBO and the Administration are in broad agreement that the two GSEs will report accounting profits on their mix of existing and new business. Instead, differences in budget estimates reflect several other factors:

- CBO projects budgetary costs for Fannie Mae and Freddie Mac because they are charging less on average for their guarantees than even the most efficient private financial institution would charge in a liquid market. The two GSEs' guarantee fees are projected to be high enough to cover expected losses and administrative expenses but not high enough to cover all of the market risk associated with the guarantees that a fully private entity would need to recover. (That situation is why analysts expect that Fannie Mae and Freddie Mac will continue to report accounting profits even if they earn lower returns than private investors would require to bear the same risks.)
- Unlike the Administration's budgetary treatment, CBO's projections cover only the costs of the two GSEs' new business. Most of the institutions' projected accounting profits will come from their existing guarantees and investment portfolios, but current and anticipated losses on the GSEs' existing portfolios and outstanding guarantees were already reported in CBO's previous baseline projections. (CBO has not reestimated those costs.)
- Because CBO considers Fannie Mae and Freddie Mac government entities for purposes of its baseline budget projections, most of the cash transactions between the two GSEs and the Treasury are treated in CBO's baseline as payments from one part of the government to another that do not affect projected deficits. (CBO makes fair-value projections for all years, including the current one, and uses them in its cost estimates. However, for certain budget projections, including those reported in its *Budget and Economic Outlook*, CBO chooses to report the cash transactions between the two GSEs and the Treasury for the current year instead of the fair-value estimate for that year. That treatment helps align CBO's deficit estimates for the current fiscal year with those of the Administration.)[16]

In CBO's judgment, using a fair-value approach rather than an alternative budgetary treatment to estimate federal subsidy costs for Fannie Mae and Freddie Mac has two principal advantages. First, by incorporating market risk, that approach provides the Congress with a more comprehensive measure of the cost of supporting the GSEs in conservatorship. Second, that approach aligns the budgetary costs with the economic costs of any eventual transition to a new model for the federal role in the secondary mortgage market. For example, sales or purchases of mortgages or MBSs by Fannie Mae or Freddie Mac that took place at competitive prices during a transition would result in neither estimated gains nor losses on a fair-value basis but might appear to have significant budgetary effects under the Administration's treatment.[17]

Thus, the choice of budgetary treatment has implications for the budgetary effects of options to attract more private capital to the secondary mortgage market and of transitions to alternative structures for that market. Although the fair-value approach would probably show small savings from a transition (depending, at least in part, on how pricing in the private mortgage market evolves relative to the guarantee fees charged by Fannie Mae and Freddie Mac), neither the cash-basis of accounting used by the Administration nor the FCRA method would report savings. Under those methods, transitioning to greater private-sector involvement in the mortgage market would most likely result in large estimated costs.

CBO's Projections for the Secondary Mortgage Market

If current policy continues and proposed regulations affecting mortgage finance are finalized as anticipated, the private mortgage market will enjoy a robust recovery over the next 10 years, CBO projects. That outlook is based on projections that the economy will continue to improve, regulatory uncertainty will be mostly resolved, house prices will rise at an average rate of about 3 percent per year in nominal terms (that is, without adjusting for the effects of inflation), and the increases in Fannie Mae's and Freddie Mac's guarantee fees that were made in 2011 and 2012 will reduce the two entities' competitive advantage. The expected return of a strong private mortgage market also depends on the anticipated recovery of the private-label MBS market or the development of alternative low-cost means of financing privately backed mortgages.

Specifically, CBO projected the following developments under current policy for the 2015–2024 period in its April 2014 baseline:[18]

- The guarantee fees charged by Fannie Mae and Freddie Mac will average 55 basis points between 2015 and 2021 and 45 basis points between 2022 (when fees are scheduled to fall by 10 basis points under current law) and 2024.[19]

- The share of new mortgages backed by the two GSEs will drop sharply, from about 60 percent in 2013 to just under 40 percent by 2021, and then increase to slightly more than 40 percent in 2022 with the scheduled decline in guarantee fees.[20] (The total dollar value of the new mortgages guaranteed by the GSEs will remain roughly stable, in nominal terms, for most of the next 10 years.)
- The subsidy rate on GSE-backed loans (the cost, expressed as a present value, to the government of each dollar of new credit guaranteed by Fannie Mae or Freddie Mac) will decline over time because of a projected drop in risk premiums for market risk.
- FHA's market share will continue to decline as private investors' willingness to insure mortgages increases.
- The private sector's market share will rise from about 20 percent in 2015 to 50 percent by 2024.
- Only a small possibility exists that a housing crisis severe enough to lead to a larger federal presence in the mortgage market will occur during the 2015– 2024 period.

The timing of the projected resurgence of private financing is subject to considerable uncertainty, which arises from many factors. For example, decisions by policy-makers about the regulatory treatment of MBSs and mortgages will affect how quickly the private mortgage market reemerges as well as its ultimate size and scope. Especially important are capital requirements for banks and risk-retention requirements for securitizers, who would have to take some losses ahead of investors in the securities. In addition, new capital standards approved by the Federal Reserve in July 2013 increased the amount of capital that banks must hold, which could make all lending slightly more costly.[21] In general, policymakers' regulatory decisions will have less effect on Fannie Mae and Freddie Mac than on their private competitors because the GSEs receive favorable regulatory treatment. However, depending on how various regulatory issues are resolved, CBO's assessment of the fair value of the GSEs' guarantees could change, as could projections of their market share. Moreover, changes in the availability of credit will help determine whether house prices grow faster or more slowly than CBO projects.

Private Market Activities

Under the Dodd-Frank Wall Street Reform and Consumer Protection Act of 2010, various federal agencies have implemented or proposed further regulations for mortgage financing. In general, those regulations are intended to strengthen incentives for making and pooling high-quality mortgages and to provide a greater cushion to absorb credit losses. The Dodd-Frank law requires lenders to verify that new borrowers have the ability to repay their loans. To comply with that requirement and classify a loan as a “qualified mortgage” under the rules recently issued by the Consumer Financial Protection Bureau, lenders consider several characteristics of the loan, including the borrower’s debt-to-income ratio, the points and fees paid by the borrower, whether the loan has risky features (interest-only loans, for example, are prohibited), and the length of the loan term (the maximum allowable term is 30 years).

Those new rules are likely to change lending practices. Lenders may be much less willing to make loans that do not meet the standards of qualified mortgages because they might face higher capital requirements on those mortgages and would face a greater risk of being sued if borrowers of those loans defaulted. One study found that only about 10 percent of the jumbo loans securitized in 2012 were made to borrowers whose debt-to-income ratios were higher than is allowed under the qualified-mortgage rules, suggesting that lenders have already become more selective.[22] In May 2013, FHFA directed Fannie Mae and Freddie Mac to purchase only loans that conform to the qualified-mortgage standards, which may further deter lenders from making loans that do not conform to those standards. In a recent Federal Reserve survey, lenders identified the ability-to-repay rules as one factor that led them to approve fewer loans for both jumbo and conforming borrowers.[23]

Another regulation, announced in October 2014, requires securitizers to retain 5 percent of the credit risk on an MBS, unless all of the loans underlying the security meet the credit standards for a qualified mortgage.[24] As long as the two GSEs remain in conservatorship and receive capital support from the government, their MBSs meet the risk-retention requirement, so the market for those securities will not be affected. Furthermore, the regulation exempts securitizations of federally insured loans, such as those backed by FHA, from the requirement. Consequently, the private-label securitization market will bear the initial impact of the requirement. Views differ about what impact that requirement will have on the availability and cost of mortgage credit.[25]

It is difficult to assess the extent to which the new rules and regulations, as opposed to other factors, are discouraging banks and other firms from issuing private-label MBSs.[26] Some observers argue that because Fannie Mae and Freddie Mac have a higher loan limit in high-cost areas than they do elsewhere, they have crowded out private financing for mortgages in those areas. The recent increase in both originations and securitizations of jumbo loans after that limit was lowered to $625,500 supports that argument. However, other observers argue that the problems with the private-label MBS market are more fundamental.[27] Investors' confidence in that market was shaken by losses experienced during the financial crisis, and they continue to be wary of the market for several reasons, including the lack of transparency about the mortgages underlying private-label securities, unreliable credit ratings, and the fact that the companies servicing mortgages have incentives that conflict with their own when loans are delinquent.

Rather than securitize mortgages, banks could hold larger amounts of loans themselves, as they have begun to do recently—albeit on a small scale—with newly originated jumbo mortgages. To help them hold larger amounts of mortgages, banks could rely more on advances (collateralized loans) from the Federal Home Loan Banks, another housing GSE. Banks might also issue covered bonds (bonds collateralized by mortgages), a type of borrowing that many large European banks use to fund the mortgages held on their balance sheets.[28] With house prices expected to trend upward, the balance sheets of lenders and investors should improve (as should borrowers' financial positions). Consequently, CBO projects that private companies will become more willing to make new loans and demand lower fees to compensate for the credit risks they take, which will reduce Fannie Mae and Freddie Mac's pricing advantage over their private competitors.

If investors' confidence is slower to return than CBO expects, the agency's projections may overestimate the recovery of the private market and the accompanying drop in federal activity (as well as the decline in the price of market risk). If, by contrast, investors' confidence recovers more quickly than expected, CBO's projections may underestimate those developments.

Changes in the GSEs' Business

If the private sector bears more mortgage credit risk, the mix of new business for Fannie Mae and Freddie Mac will probably be affected. CBO expects that as market risk premiums decline over time, lenders will keep—or sell to securitizers in the private-label market—more of the mortgages taken out by borrowers with high credit scores and large down payments, most of which are currently backed by the two GSEs. (Similarly, under its current fee structure, FHA will probably lose its safest borrowers to private lenders over time.) In CBO's baseline projections, the agency anticipates that Fannie Mae's and Freddie Mac's mix of new business will become riskier as the least risky mortgages are backed by private firms.

Recent developments provide some support for CBO's expectations about the private market. Data show that some banks are starting to hold more of their safest conforming loans rather than paying guarantee fees to Fannie Mae and Freddie Mac.

SECTION 2. OPTIONS FOR ATTRACTING MORE PRIVATE CAPITAL TO THE SECONDARY MORTGAGE MARKET

Policymakers are considering a range of proposals to restructure the mortgage finance system, most of which call for shrinking or eventually eliminating Fannie Mae and Freddie Mac and fostering greater participation by the private sector. Even without policy changes, the private sector's role is expected to grow over time as the effects of the financial crisis fade. However, private companies face some barriers to participating fully in the mortgage finance system, most notably Fannie Mae's and Freddie Mac's below-market guarantee fees. The government-sponsored enterprises guarantee all or most of the credit risk on eligible mortgages, and the size limit for eligible mortgages is high enough to encompass most of the mortgage market. This Section examines several mechanisms that policymakers could use to attract more private capital to the secondary mortgage market. (The various ways in which those mechanisms can be combined to help transition the market to a new structure are addressed in Section 3.)

To encourage a larger private role in the secondary market, policymakers could pursue several approaches:[1]

- Raise the guarantee fees charged by Fannie Mae and Freddie Mac to lessen the pricing advantage that those institutions receive as a result of their federal backing;
- Change eligible loan limits—either reduce loan limits to decrease the share of the mortgage market that the two GSEs are allowed to guarantee or increase loan limits to complement other policy changes;

- Require the GSEs to share credit risk with the private sector so that private investors would bear some of the losses when mortgages went into default; and
- Limit the GSEs' role by using a competitive process, such as auctions, to provide a certain quantity of mortgage guarantees to the highest bidders.

Regulators already have the power to proceed with those approaches, although the Congressional Budget Office's baseline projections for Fannie Mae and Freddie Mac incorporate the assumption that current fee levels and loan limits will persist and that risk sharing will remain limited. (In the baseline, guarantee fees drop by 10 basis points in 2022 with the scheduled expiration of the fee increase enacted in the Temporary Payroll Tax Cut Continuation Act of 2011.)

How those mechanisms would be used would vary depending on the new structure for the secondary mortgage market that policymakers wanted to put in place. Some commentators view changes in guarantee fees and loan limits as necessary first steps in moving toward any market structure with a reduced federal presence.[2] Risk sharing and auctions are well suited to creating market structures that would retain a federal presence but alter federal guarantees, either by restricting the scope of the guarantees (so they covered fewer mortgages or only catastrophic losses) or by making the guarantees widely available only during times of financial stress.

For each of the four mechanisms listed above, CBO examined several alternative options and estimated their impact on the federal government's subsidy costs for Fannie Mae and Freddie Mac starting in 2015. Almost all of the options would result in some savings to the federal budget. CBO also evaluated the options' likely effects on credit availability, mortgage interest rates, house prices, and the burden of risk borne by taxpayers. Additionally, the options would affect the Federal Housing Administration's activities by causing some borrowers to shift to mortgages insured by FHA instead of by the private market. (Because the amount of FHA's new guarantees is controlled through appropriation acts, lawmakers would have to raise the limit on new guarantees for that shift to occur. The budgetary effects on FHA from such a shift would be relatively modest under most of the options; those effects are not included in CBO's estimates.)

Raise Guarantee Fees

In recent years, the Federal Housing Finance Agency has twice raised Fannie Mae's and Freddie Mac's guarantee fees on new loans by 10 basis points, and lawmakers have increased fees by an additional 10 basis points. In January 2014, those fees averaged about 55 basis points (0.55 percentage points) of a loan's unpaid principal. (The estimates in this report are based on that 55 basis-point average, but the average fee has risen to around 60 basis points over the first six months of 2014 as the composition of loans has changed to include relatively more higher-risk and fewer lower-risk loans.) Policy-makers could continue to increase the two GSEs' guarantee fees to attract new private capital to the secondary market. Those fees are passed along to borrowers, so an increase of 10 basis points in the GSEs' guarantee fees would raise interest rates on mortgages by about 10 basis points.

Analysts disagree about how much those fees would need to rise to attract significantly greater amounts of private capital, and the answer depends in part on regulatory rules that have not yet been finalized.[3] Because of the high credit quality of some of the GSEs' new loans, CBO anticipates that even a small increase in guarantee fees from the present level would allow private firms to immediately compete for the highest-quality loans. The resulting decline in new guarantees by Fannie Mae and Freddie Mac would grow over time, CBO estimates, as the risk premiums that private firms charged for assuming credit risk declined. Larger fee increases would probably be needed, however, before private firms could compete for lower-quality loans currently purchased by the two GSEs. Those loans are made to high-risk borrowers, who either make smaller down payments or have lower credit scores than the typical borrower whose mortgage is guaranteed by the GSEs.

Options

To illustrate a range of possible outcomes, CBO estimated the potential savings and other effects of three options for permanently raising the guarantee fees charged by Fannie Mae and Freddie Mac above the levels projected under current policy (55 basis points through 2021 and 45 basis points thereafter):[4]

- An increase of 10 basis points beginning in 2015;
- An increase of 20 basis points phased in over two years (10 basis points in 2015 and another 10 basis points beginning in 2016); and

- An increase of 50 basis points spread over the 2015– 2024 period (with a 5 basis-point rise each year).

Those increases are assumed to be assessed uniformly on borrowers whose mortgages are purchased by the two GSEs. To keep fees from dropping after 2021, when the 10 basis-point rise that took effect in 2011 is set to expire, the options would be coupled with a permanent extension of that increase.

Effects on the GSEs' Subsidy Costs and New Guarantees

CBO's estimates show that even relatively small increases in guarantee fees would have a large impact on the federal government's subsidy costs for Fannie Mae and Freddie Mac. For example, an increase of 10 basis points would reduce subsidy costs over the 2015–2024 period by $10 billion—or more than half of the subsidy costs that CBO projects for the two GSEs during that period under current policy (see Table 2-1). (By itself, a permanent extension of the 10 basis-point rise in fees enacted in 2011 would reduce subsidies by $3 billion through 2024.) The timing of fee increases would affect the subsidy estimates, but under all three of the options, subsidy costs for Fannie Mae and Freddie Mac would drop to about $100 million a year or less by 2024.

A 10 basis-point increase in guarantee fees would also decrease the volume of new loan guarantees by the two GSEs by $3.1 trillion (23 percent) over the 2015–2024 period, CBO estimates. Among the fee increases that CBO examined, the gradual 50 basis-point rise would have the greatest impact on the GSEs' new loan guarantees—reducing them by $7.4 trillion (55 percent) over the 2015–2024 period. That option would leave Fannie Mae and Freddie Mac guaranteeing less than $200 billion of new loans by 2024 (see Figure 2-1).

CBO's estimates of subsidy costs and new guarantees reflect the shift that higher guarantee fees would bring about in the mix of borrowers whose loans are purchased by the two GSEs as lower-risk borrowers increasingly turned to private lenders, leaving the GSEs holding predominantly loans of higher-risk borrowers. Such a shift is also expected to occur at current fee levels as the private securitization market recovers, but fee increases would accelerate it. The change in the composition of loan purchases would occur because Fannie Mae's and Freddie Mac's fee structures do not fully reflect differences in the riskiness of borrowers, despite the fact that they charge different fees for different kinds of mortgages.[5] In CBO's estimation, it is that change in the mix of borrowers that would prevent subsidies from being completely eliminated by raising fees. The differential effects of fee increases on different types of borrowers could become less important, however, if Fannie Mae and Freddie Mac continued to improve their risk-based pricing.

CBO estimates that the guarantee fees currently being paid by the GSEs' highest-quality borrowers, who make large down payments and have high credit ratings, are close to the fees that private insurers would charge those borrowers. Thus, CBO estimates that even relatively modest fee increases would reduce the volume of new GSE guarantees to some extent. However, reducing the volume of new GSE guarantees substantially in the short term would require a notable rise in fees because risk premiums on privately backed mortgages are expected to remain high for some time. Some market analysts argue that an increase of at least 20 basis points in the GSEs' fees might be necessary to shift a significant amount of loan guarantee business to the private sector in the short term, until the private securitization market recovers further and risk premiums drop.[6] If that view is correct, Fannie Mae and Freddie Mac might see little loss in business or change in the mix of borrowers in the next year or two from fee increases in the range of 10 basis points to 20 basis points, even though their business might decline significantly in later years. If, however, the private market recovers faster than anticipated, the volume of new GSE guarantees could fall more sharply than expected in the near term from such fee increases.

Change Loan Limits

Some analysts argue that high dollar limits for conforming mortgages have crowded out private financing and that lower limits are a precondition for more private activity in the secondary market.[7] Currently, the statutory limit on the size of single-family mortgages that Fannie Mae and Freddie Mac are allowed to purchase is $417,000 in most areas. In response to a sharp falloff in the availability of private financing during the financial crisis, lawmakers temporarily allowed the two GSEs to buy and guarantee mortgages up to $729,750 in areas with high housing costs. That high-cost limit fell to $625,500 in October 2011, and private markets have since taken over the financing of most new mortgages between that and the previous limit. Data show that in 2012, originations of privately backed jumbo loans rose by nearly 20 percent, to $200 billion, while the number of jumbo loans insured by FHA, whose loan limit in high-cost areas was still $729,750, rose only slightly.[8] (FHA's loan limit fell to $625,500 in 2014.)

Table 2-1. Effects of Various Options for Attracting Private Capital to the Secondary Mortgage Market on Projected Fair-Value Subsidy Costs and GSE Loan Guarantees, 2015 to 2024

(Billions of dollars)		
	Federal Subsidy Costs for the GSEs[a]	Amount of New Loan Guarantees by the GSEs
	CBO's Baseline	
Current Policy	19	13,500
	Effects of Raising the GSEs' Guarantee Fees[b]	
Fees raised by 10 basis points in 2015	-10	-3,100
2 Fees raised by 20 basis points (10 points in 2015 and 10 in 2016)	-15	-5,300
Fees raised by 50 basis points (5 points per year from 2015 to 2024)	-11	-7,400
	Effects of Changing the GSEs' Loan Limits	
Limits lowered to $417,000 by 2016	*	-700
Limits lowered to $150,000 by 2024	-4	-4,500
Limits lowered to zero by 2024	-5	-6,100
Limits raised to $729,750 in 2015	**	100
	Effects of Sharing Credit Risk[b,c]	
Private parties take first losses of up to 10 percent of loan balance, and guarantee fees raised by 10 basis points	-10	-3,100
Private parties take first losses of up to 20 percent of loan balance, and guarantee fees raised by 10 basis points	-10	-3,100
	Effects of Introducing Auctions for New GSE Guara ntees	
GSEs' share of the market for new mortgages reduced to 25 percent by 2024	-10	-2,400

(Billions of dollars)		
	Federal Subsidy Costs for the GSEsa	Amount of New Loan Guarantees by the GSEs
GSEs' share of the market for new mortgages reduced to 10 percent by 2024	-11	-4,400

Source: Congressional Budget Office.

Notes: A basis point is 0.01 percentage point.

GSEs = government-sponsored enterprises (specifically, Fannie Mae and Freddie Mac); * = between zero and $500 million; ** = between -$500 million and zero.

[a] Excludes potential effects on federal spending for the Federal Housing Administration (FHA) and the Government National Mortgage Association (Ginnie Mae). Spending on those agencies is set through annual appropriation acts and thus is classified as discretionary spending, whereas spending on Fannie Mae and Freddie Mac is not determined by appropriation acts and thus is classified as mandatory spending. In addition, FHA's annual commitments for new guarantees of single-family mortgages are subject to a limit set each year.

[b] To avoid a drop in guarantee fees starting in fiscal year 2022, these options would permanently extend the 10 basis-point increase in the GSEs' guarantee fees enacted in the Temporary Payroll Tax Cut Continuation Act of 2011, which is due to expire on October 1, 2021. That extension by itself would reduce subsidies through 2024 by $3 billion.

[c] Estimated changes are the same for both options because those changes result from the rise of 10 basis points in guarantee fees that CBO assumed would accompany either risk-sharing option. The risk sharing itself would have little to no effect on subsidy costs or guarantees because the compensation that the GSEs would have to pay private investors to assume credit risk would generally match the benefit that the GSEs would derive from shedding that risk. However, CBO assumed that the GSEs would pass some of their costs of compensating investors on to mortgage borrowers in the form of higher guarantee fees.

The Federal Housing Finance Agency is considering reducing loan limits for Fannie Mae and Freddie Mac from $417,000 to $400,000 in most areas and from $625,500 to $600,000 in high-cost areas. Those lower limits would still be much larger than most of the mortgages guaranteed by the two GSEs. For example, in the first eight months of 2011 (a period for which more detailed data were available to CBO), about 80 percent of the mortgages guaranteed by Fannie Mae and Freddie Mac were smaller than $300,000, and over half were smaller than $200,000 (see Figure 2-2). Although the average size of those guarantees has risen since then, a reduction in the GSEs' loan limits would have to be large to have a significant impact on the secondary mortgage market.

Alternatively, an increase in loan limits might be desirable as a complement to other changes designed to increase private financing. The rationale for such a combination of changes is discussed in the next Section.

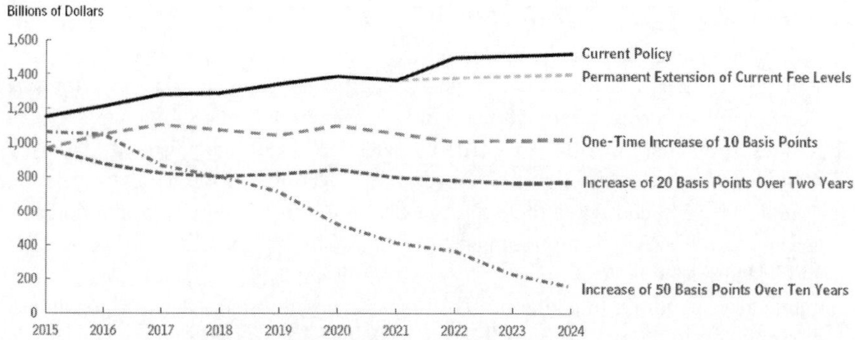

Source: Congressional Budget Office.

Note: Under current policy, the 10 basis-point (0.1 percentage-point) increase in Fannie Mae's and Freddie Mac's guarantee fees that was authorized by the Temporary Payroll Tax Cut Continuation Act of 2011 is due to expire on October 1, 2021, which causes CBO's baseline projection of new guarantees to jump in 2022. All of the options for changing the guarantee fees include the permanent extension of that 10 basis-point increase.

Figure 2-1. Volume of New Loan Guarantees by Fannie Mae and Freddie Mac Under Different Options for Changing Their Guarantee Fees.

Options

CBO analyzed several options for changing the size limits for conforming mortgages:

- Reducing the loan limit for high-cost areas to $500,000 in 2015 and then to $417,000—the level that existed before the financial crisis—in 2016 and thereafter.
- Gradually reducing the loan limits for all areas to $150,000 by 2024. That amount is about $20,000 lower than the mortgage that a borrower who made a 20 percent down payment would need to purchase an existing home at the median price of about $210,000 in October 2014.

- Gradually reducing the loan limits for all areas to zero. Limits would fall to $417,000 by 2016 and then decline steadily, by about $50,000 a year, until the limit reached zero in 2024, at which point the GSEs could not make any new guarantees.
- Raising the loan limits for all areas to $729,750 beginning in 2015.

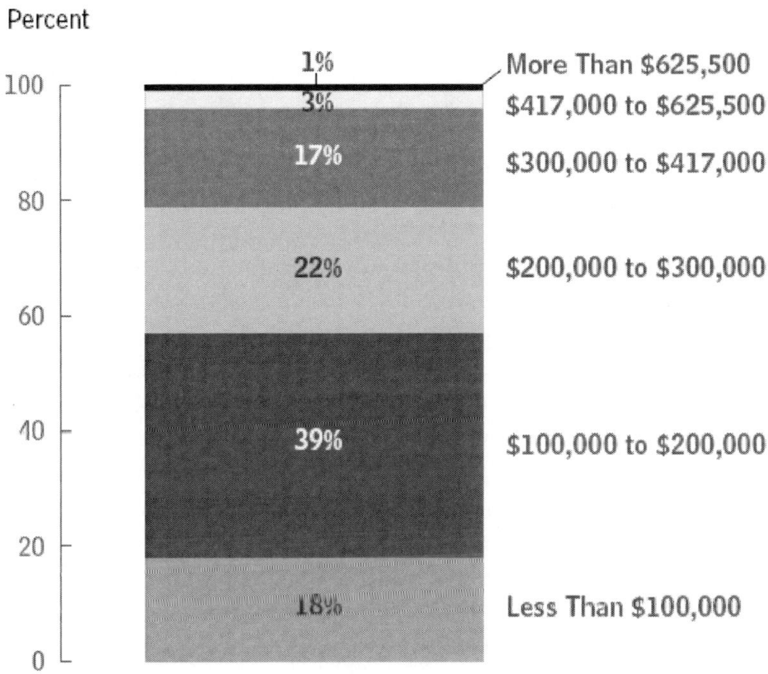

Source: Congressional Budget Office based on data from the Federal Housing Finance Agency.

Note: This percentage distribution is based on the total number of mortgages guaranteed by Fannie Mae and Freddie Mac rather than the total dollar amount of those mortgages.

Figure 2-2. Distribution of Fannie Mae and Freddie Mac's Calendar Year 2011 Guarantees, by Size of the Mortgage at Origination.

Effects on the GSEs' Subsidy Costs and New Guarantees

In general, deeper reductions in loan limits would produce larger savings in federal subsidy costs for Fannie Mae and Freddie Mac. CBO estimates that those costs would fall by a total of about $5 billion between 2015 and 2024 if loan limits gradually declined to zero and by $4 billion over that period if loan limits gradually fell to $150,000 (see Table 2-1 on page 22).

CBO's estimates of the impact of altering loan limits take into account changes in the credit risks posed by mortgage borrowers. In general, the creditworthiness of borrowers rises with the size of mortgages, up to some ceiling. Beyond that level, creditworthiness declines, perhaps because borrowers are stretching themselves financially to buy bigger homes. CBO's initial analysis suggests that borrowers with mortgage balances between $417,000 and $625,500 tend to be more creditworthy as a group than other borrowers.

Thus, if loan limits were lowered to $417,000, subsidy costs would probably rise rather than fall (at least initially), CBO estimates, because the two GSEs would likely lose their most profitable group of borrowers and retain their more costly borrowers, who buy lower-priced homes. Raising loan limits to $729,750 would slightly reduce subsidy costs because borrowers at that level probably pose lower-than-average credit risks.

By altering the share of mortgages that Fannie Mae and Freddie Mac are allowed to buy, changes in loan limits would also affect the volume of new loan guarantees that the institutions make each year. That volume would fall or rise in tandem with the loan limits under the four options. New GSE guarantees, and the accompanying subsidies, would be eliminated by 2024 if loan limits declined to zero (see Figure 2-3).

Share Credit Risk with the Private Sector

Shifting some of the responsibility for losses from defaults to the private sector is another way to reduce the federal government's role in the secondary mortgage market. In 2013, the Federal Housing Finance Agency required Fannie Mae and Freddie Mac to each initiate new risk-sharing transactions worth $30 billion as part of a transition to a more private market.[9] Both GSEs have completed multiple transactions, and the success of those transactions has encouraged FHFA to increase the goal to $90 billion for 2014 (see the appendix for more details).[10] The GSEs were already shifting some credit risk to the private sector. For example, their charters mandate that they require private mortgage insurance (or another form of credit enhancement) on single-family loans with down payments of less than 20 percent. In 2013, less than 20 percent of the new loans guaranteed by Fannie Mae and Freddie Mac were covered by private mortgage insurance or some other form of credit enhancement. Such insurance covers a fixed portion of the losses on the unpaid principal of a mortgage but not the entire mortgage—for example, coverage is generally 25 percent of the loan balance for a 30-year fixed rate mortgage that has a loan-to-value ratio of 90 percent.

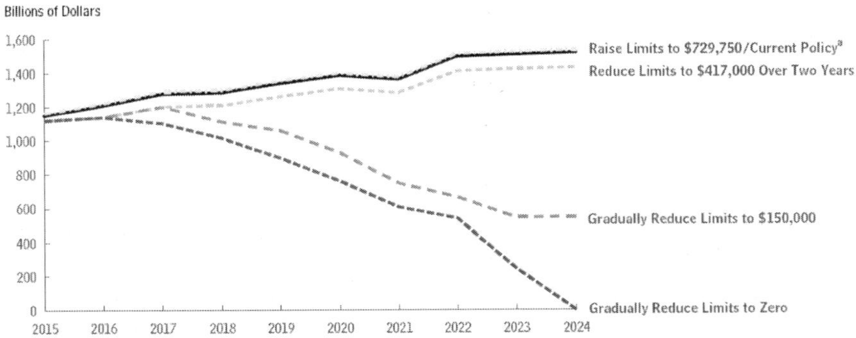

Source: Congressional Budget Office.

Note: Under current policy, the increase in guarantee fees of 10 basis points (0.1 percentage point) that was authorized by the Temporary Payroll Tax Cut Continuation Act of 2011 is due to expire on October 1, 2021, which causes CBO's baseline projection of new guarantees to jump in 2022.

[a] Raising the loan limits to $727,750 would increase guarantees by an average of less than $10 billion a year; thus, the line for that option is nearly indistinguishable from the line for current policy.

Figure 2-3. Volume of New Loan Guarantees by Fannie Mae and Freddie Mac Under Different Options for Changing Their Loan Limits.

The two GSEs routinely spread credit risk to a greater extent on mortgages made to owners of multifamily properties. With such loans, Fannie Mae generally requires lenders to share the credit risk of the loans pooled into mortgage-backed securities—for example, by bearing the first 5 percent of credit losses on a loan and then sharing losses equally with Fannie Mae up to a limit. Freddie Mac takes an alternative approach: It issues multifamily MBSs that are not fully guaranteed. If a borrower defaults, investors who bought the securities must absorb a certain amount of the losses before Freddie Mac bears any.

Fannie Mae and Freddie Mac could use a variety of approaches to share the credit risk on their single-family MBSs with the private sector: They could issue securities that do not carry a full GSE guarantee, purchase insurance against credit losses, or require borrowers to obtain more private mortgage insurance. Under such arrangements, private entities or investors would be responsible for some losses before the GSEs and taxpayers were, and the two GSEs would effectively be transferring some of their guarantee income to compensate those private entities or investors for bearing those risks. The different arrangements might have different transaction costs and may vary in terms of private investors' willingness to take part in them, but, in principle, all of them could achieve a desired level of risk sharing with the private sector. CBO's analysis is based on a generic risk-sharing approach and does not account for the differences between various possible methods (which are discussed in the appendix). For example, although some risk-sharing approaches could directly change the amount of new GSE guarantees, CBO's estimates do not reflect that possibility.

Risk could be shared on the basis of either individual loans or a pool of loans. That choice would have different implications for taxpayers and investors. On a pool of loans, for example, private investors might agree to cover the first 10 percent of losses, regardless of how those losses were spread among the individual loans.[11] Thus, if the pool contained $1 billion of loans, private investors would be responsible for the first $100 million of losses, and taxpayers would be responsible for the remainder. By contrast, if investors had to provide private mortgage insurance covering the first 10 percent of the credit risk on individual loans, they would be responsible for the first $100 million of losses only if all of the loans in the pool lost at least 10 percent, which would be unlikely. With that risk-sharing arrangement, taxpayers would bear more, and investors less, of the potential losses than they would with pool-based risk sharing.

Options

The different risk-sharing mechanisms—issuing securities that do not carry a full GSE guarantee, purchasing insurance against credit losses, or requiring borrowers to obtain more private mortgage insurance—could be used to transfer various amounts of credit risk to private parties. Those private parties would either be investors in the unguaranteed portion of the MBSs issued by Fannie Mae and Freddie Mac, insurance companies selling credit protection tied to the performance of a pool of GSE-backed loans, or private mortgage insurers selling protection to borrowers. CBO analyzed two alternative levels of sharing the GSEs' credit risk with the private sector:

- Private parties would be responsible for losses of up to 10 percent of the principal amount of a qualifying mortgage pooled into any new MBS issued by Fannie Mae or Freddie Mac, or

- Private parties would be responsible for losses of up to 20 percent of the principal amount of a qualifying mortgage pooled into any new MBS issued by Fannie Mae or Freddie Mac.

For both options, CBO assumed that the two GSEs would pass along some of the cost of the risk sharing to borrowers. Although the process for doing that would differ according to the particular risk-sharing mechanism used, borrowers would effectively be paying higher guarantee fees. Consequently, federal subsidies would decline.

In both options, risk sharing would apply at the loan level rather than the pool level. For example, on a loan with an unpaid principal balance of $200,000 and risk sharing of up to 10 percent of that balance, private parties would bear the first $20,000 of credit losses, and Fannie Mae or Freddie Mac would bear the rest. Losses on the GSEs' newly guaranteed mortgages that end up in default are projected to average roughly 25 percent over the next several years, meaning that the losses on a $200,000 loan in default would average $50,000, of which private parties would bear $20,000, and Fannie Mae or Freddie Mac would bear the remaining $30,000. If, as in the second option, private parties were liable for losses of up to 20 percent of the loan balance, they would bear $40,000 of the $50,000 losses, and the GSEs would be responsible for $10,000.

CBO expects that there would be enough competition among private parties to participate in such risk-sharing arrangements that the transfer of risk would occur at a cost close to the fair value of the risk. With risk sharing of up to 10 percent on each loan, private parties would require compensation equal to about 14 basis points, on average, to cover their expected losses and to provide an appropriate premium for market risk, CBO estimates. The amount that they charged for covering losses of up to 20 percent of a loan balance would be slightly more than twice that amount because as investors bore the risk of deeper losses, they would also assume a bigger share of the market risk. If the GSEs incurred large administrative and legal costs in those risk-sharing transactions, the total costs of the transactions could be slightly higher than fair value. (As explained below, whether those costs affected federal subsidies for the GSEs would depend on whether the GSEs passed them on to mortgage borrowers.)

As conditions in housing and financial markets evolved over time, the price that private investors would charge to assume some of the GSEs' credit risk would also change. Consequently, under these two options, Fannie Mae and Freddie Mac would be allowed to adjust their guarantee fees whenever the cost of risk sharing shifted. That flexibility would make fees and interest rates on GSE-backed mortgages more volatile but would keep federal subsidies fairly stable.

Effects on the GSEs' Subsidy Costs and New Guarantees

If Fannie Mae and Freddie Mac transferred credit risk in transactions that occurred at fair value, risk sharing would have little or no effect on the federal government's subsidy costs for the two GSEs. That would be the case regardless of the amount of risk shared: If the transactions occurred at fair value, the benefit that the GSEs derived from shedding some credit risk would exactly offset the price they paid private investors for assuming that risk. In other words, the income from guarantee fees that they passed on to private investors as compensation would be balanced by the reduction in the cost of their expected losses.

Federal subsidies would decline, however, if the price that private entities charged for risk sharing encouraged the two GSEs to reduce the extent to which they subsidized mortgage borrowers. If, for example, the GSEs raised guarantee fees by 10 basis points (and permanently extended the 10 basis-point increase enacted in the Temporary Payroll Tax Cut Continuation Act of 2011 that expires in 2021) in conjunction with the risk-sharing initiatives, federal subsidy costs would be $10 billion lower over the 2015–2024 period than they would be under current policy, CBO estimates (see Table 2-1 on page 22). That reduction from the 10 basis-point increase in guarantee fees would be the same whether the amount of risk being shared was 10 percent of a loan's balance or 20 percent. Although CBO assumed a 10 basis-point fee increase for these options, the GSEs could change the amount of the investor-compensation costs they passed on to borrowers as the fair value of the transactions changed with market conditions and the cost of risk sharing. By 2024, annual subsidy costs for Fannie Mae and Freddie Mac would be about $100 million under both options, and the two GSEs would guarantee about $1 trillion of new loans annually.

The higher guarantee fees under those options would encourage some borrowers to seek private alternatives. As a result, CBO estimates, the volume of new guarantees by Fannie Mae and Freddie Mac would drop by $3.1 trillion (about 23 percent) over the 2015–2024 period. For that estimate, CBO anticipates that all of the change in the volume of GSE guarantees would stem from higher guarantee fees, so the change would be the same whether the GSEs shed 10 percent or 20 percent of their risk.[12]

CBO's estimates of savings from the risk-sharing options take into account the possibility that in some instances a portion of the risk shed by Fannie Mae and Freddie Mac could come back to them in the form of counterparty risk—the chance that other parties to a transaction will not be able to meet their obligations. For example, if the two GSEs required more private insurance coverage for some mortgages, it is possible that the private insurers could default on their obligations. Because such counter-party risk would lessen the extent to which these risk-sharing options would reduce federal subsidy costs, CBO incorporates that risk into its estimates.

The biggest advantage of sharing more credit risk with the private sector is that Fannie Mae's or Freddie Mac's expected losses from a default on a mortgage would drop significantly, which would directly reduce the government's exposure to risk. In addition, as long as the mechanism for shifting risk was transparent and the process was competitive, the prices paid in those transactions would give regulators and lawmakers additional signals about the cost of mortgage risk. One major potential disadvantage of sharing credit risk with the private sector is that doing so would increase private parties' systemic risk—the risk that those parties' failure could be detrimental to the financial system and the economy. The magnitude of that change in systemic risk would vary, depending on the particular risk-sharing approach used.

Use Auctions to Limit Guarantees

Policymakers could control the size of the GSEs' role in the market by requiring Fannie Mae and Freddie Mac to use an auction process to provide guarantees on limited quantities of new mortgages. Using an auction mechanism to determine which mortgages would be guaranteed and securitized would replace the current approach— guaranteeing all eligible loans submitted by lenders at predetermined fee levels. Auctions offer the potential advantage of indicating the market price of mortgage risk more accurately than regulators can estimate that price. In addition, auctions would allocate the GSEs' guarantees to the eligible lenders that placed the most value on having their loans guaranteed.

Fannie Mae and Freddie Mac could periodically auction off a limited number of guarantees that might cover 100 percent of the credit risk associated with a mortgage. Under such a process, the GSEs would announce the number of mortgages they would guarantee, as well as any other restrictions they might have, and lenders would submit bids indicating how much they would pay to have their pools of mortgages guaranteed. Lenders would be willing to bid on the guarantees because loans that were not federally backed would have to be either held on their balance sheets or securitized privately at greater cost. The size of the auctions would control the GSEs' exposure to risk, and the eligibility requirements would determine how broad a range of mortgages could be guaranteed. The auctions would be held periodically to allow the quantity and price of the GSEs' guarantees to adjust to market conditions.

In an efficient auction, the winning bidders for credit guarantees would be the financial institutions that placed the highest value on those guarantees. Because the bidders would have diverse pools of loans with different degrees of riskiness, such auctions could pose a challenge. If the auction mechanism failed to control for differences in risk, Fannie Mae and Freddie Mac could end up with the riskiest loans in the bidding pool without receiving adequate compensation for their guarantees. Auctions could control for observable differences in credit risk among loans, however, by using a predetermined set of publicly announced criteria that were based on such characteristics as loan-to-value ratio, the borrower's credit score, the size of the loan, and its maturity. Under such an auction process, the institutions that incurred larger costs from holding certain types of mortgages would be willing to pay more to have those mortgages guaranteed and thus would submit higher bids. Consequently, if the auction process was properly designed, it would cause Fannie Mae and Freddie Mac to guarantee loans from the financial institutions that valued such guarantees the most rather than just guaranteeing the pools of loans with the highest risks.[13]

Options

CBO analyzed two options for using auctions to control the size of the GSEs' role in the secondary mortgage market. Under either option, Fannie Mae and Freddie Mac would determine which mortgages to guarantee and at what price by periodically auctioning off a set amount of guarantees. The GSEs would auction off progressively smaller amounts over time.

The two options differ in the extent of the decrease in the GSEs' share of the mortgage market:

- Phasing in a reduction in the GSEs' share of the mortgage market to 25 percent by 2024, or
- Phasing in a reduction in the GSEs' share of the mortgage market to 10 percent by 2024.

Unlike the other options discussed in this Section, which would begin in 2015, the auctions would not be fully implemented until 2016. CBO incorporated a one-year delay because the auctions might need to be tested on a small scale before becoming a major part of the GSEs' operations.

Effects on the GSEs' Subsidy Costs and New Guarantees

Reducing the share of new mortgages guaranteed by Fannie Mae and Freddie Mac from over 60 percent in 2013 to much lower percentages would significantly decrease the federal government's subsidies for the two GSEs. CBO estimates that subsidy costs over the 2015– 2024 period would be $10 billion lower if the GSEs' market share gradually declined to 25 percent—or $11 billion lower if their market share declined to 10 percent— than those costs would be under current policy (see Table 2-1 on page 22). The volume of new loans guaranteed by Fannie Mae and Freddie Mac during that period would be reduced by 18 percent under the first option and by 33 percent under the second option (see Figure 2-4).

Although bids in a competitive auction could be high enough to eliminate government subsidies for loan guarantees, CBO anticipates, for several reasons, that most of the auctions through 2024 would yield bids that involve some degree of subsidy. The auctions would sell a relatively large number of guarantees in the early years, which would reduce competition for the last guarantee and deter firms from bidding at a level that involved no subsidy. (As the amount of guarantees declined over time and auctions became more competitive, firms would probably bid more aggressively, and bids would approach a non-subsidized level.) Another reason some subsidies might persist is that mortgage markets arc fairly concentrated and dominated by a small number of large banks; thus, some auctions would not be highly competitive, particularly if certain banks specialized in a type of mortgage available for guarantee. In addition, subsidies might persist because of unobserved differences in the mortgage pools being guaranteed. (Over time, however, the auction mechanism might correct for those unobserved differences.)

CBO expects that bidding in the auctions would raise Fannie Mae's and Freddie Mac's guarantee fees in the first few years by up to 5 basis points, pushing them closer to fair-value levels. Because bids would probably be more aggressive if fewer guarantees were available, guarantee fees on individual loans would most likely be slightly higher under the option that aimed for a 10 percent market share in 2024 than under the option with a 25 percent target. Fees might rise by less if the auction process was poorly designed or if only a few firms participated.

CBO's estimates do not take into account any delays or difficulties that could arise in setting up the auctions.

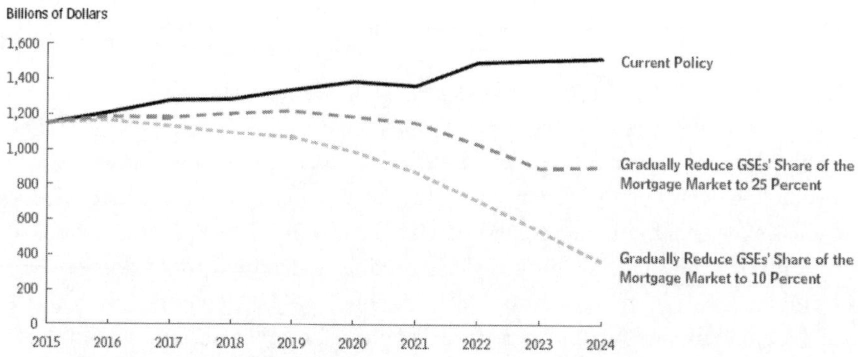

Source: Congressional Budget Office.

Notes: Under current policy, the increase in guarantee fees of 10 basis points (0.1 percentage point) that was authorized by the Temporary Payroll Tax Cut Continuation Act of 2011 is due to expire on October 1, 2021, which causes CBO's baseline projection of new guarantees to jump in 2022.

These options would not begin until 2016, to allow time for any implementation issues with auctions of the GSEs' guarantees to be resolved.

GSEs = government-sponsored enterprises (specifically, Fannie Mae and Freddie Mac).

Figure 2-4. Volume of New Loan Guarantees by Fannie Mae and Freddie Mac Under Different Options for Auctioning Their Guarantees.

Broader Effects of the Options on the Housing Market and Taxpayers

Compared with current policy, reducing the federal presence in the secondary mortgage market would reduce federal subsidies for mortgages. As a result, that approach would probably make credit less available, raise interest rates on mortgages, put downward pressure on house prices, and decrease the amount of credit risk borne by taxpayers. The continued availability of mortgages insured by FHA would provide a safety net for borrowers whom the private market was unwilling to serve at an affordable cost.

Mortgage Interest Rates and Availability of Credit

Raising Fannie Mae's and Freddie Mac's guarantee fees and sharing credit risk would increase the cost of credit because the higher fees paid by lenders would probably be passed on to mortgage borrowers in the form of higher interest rates. The effects on most borrowers would be modest, however. For example, if fees rose by 20 basis points, the monthly payment on a 30-year fixed rate loan of $200,000 would increase by $25 a month. Borrowers would still have access to credit, although at a higher cost. In contrast, auctioning the guarantees would both raise the cost of credit and reduce its availability.

Reducing Fannie Mae's and Freddie Mac's loan limits would raise the cost of credit and possibly lessen its availability for mortgages between the current and new limits. In the short run, interest rates for most borrowers of such mortgages could be higher than the rates on jumbo loans (which were up to 50 basis points higher than the rates on GSE-backed loans in 2013 but were generally less than 10 basis points higher than those rates in the first 11 months of 2014). Most of the affected borrowers would pay more than the jumbo rate because they are less creditworthy than the typical borrower of a jumbo loan. Currently, lenders generally require borrowers in the jumbo market to make larger down payments and have higher credit scores than the average borrower of a conforming loan. The premiums charged by private mortgage insurers also imply that those borrowers would face higher mortgage interest rates. If rate increases ranged between 10 basis points and 50 basis points, the monthly payment on a 30-year fixed rate loan of $500,000 would rise between $30 and $150. Rate increases on jumbo loans would probably be lower over the long run as more private capital entered the secondary market and mortgage risk premiums fell. Less creditworthy borrowers would probably face even larger increases in interest rates if they qualified for private-sector financing.[14]

House Prices

Changes in interest rates can affect the price of housing through several channels—with potentially opposite effects—but the net impact is that higher rates generally put downward pressure on house prices.[15] Higher interest rates lead to higher monthly mortgage payments, potentially reducing the size of loans for which borrowers could qualify.[16] Those forces reduce the demand for housing and thereby cause house prices to decline or to grow less quickly than they would if interest rates were lower. At the same time, however, changes in interest rates can affect the supply of housing by altering developers' financing costs, the amount of new construction, and expectations about future growth in house prices.

CBO cannot confidently predict the extent to which higher interest rates might push down house prices under any of the options discussed in this Section because estimates of how sensitive such prices are to changes in interest rates are uncertain and vary with financial conditions. Estimates of the decline in house prices following a rise of 1 percentage point in the real (inflation-adjusted) interest rate range from as little as 1 percent to as much as 8 percent in the medium term.[17] (In the long run, the decline in prices is likely to be smaller as the supply of housing adjusts to higher interest rates by contracting.) Consequently, if interest rates for homebuyers borrowing more than the proposed loan limits rose by 25 basis points, prices for the homes that such borrowers typically purchase would be expected to appreciate between 0.25 percent and 2 percent more slowly than under current policy.

Reducing loan limits would have a larger impact on home prices in areas with high housing costs, such as California, than it would in lower-cost areas. If policymakers wanted such a change to have more uniform effects, they could allow Fannie Mae's and Freddie Mac's loan limits to vary with local house prices, as FHA's loan limits and the two GSEs' limits in high-cost areas currently do. Although setting such variable limits would mute the effects on high-cost areas, many lower-cost parts of the country could see sizable drops in their limits for conforming mortgages.

Financial Risks to Taxpayers

Encouraging the private sector to play a larger role in the secondary mortgage market would reduce taxpayers' exposure to risk from Fannie Mae's and Freddie Mac's activities. Taxpayers would still face some risk, however, from the federal safety net that covers banks and other large financial institutions. That safety net includes federal deposit insurance and any implicit guarantees that the federal government will come to the aid of major financial institutions—as it did during the most recent financial crisis. That aid protected many uninsured creditors of large financial institutions from losses and supported the continued availability of credit to households and businesses, though at great potential costs to taxpayers.

More stringent regulations (such as those stemming from the Dodd-Frank Act of 2010 and included in the proposed Basel III international agreement) are expected to impose higher capital requirements on large banks. Those regulations might better protect taxpayers from the risks of such banks' failures by reducing both the probability and the cost of those failures.[18]

Because large banks hold more diversified portfolios of assets and more capital than do Fannie Mae and Freddie Mac, they may pose less risk to taxpayers than do the two GSEs. Moreover, community banks and other small institutions might take on some of the mortgage risk from the GSEs without much risk to taxpayers.

FHA Guarantees

CBO expects that most mortgage borrowers who would no longer qualify for loans backed by the GSEs under these options would opt for private-sector financing instead. However, some would choose, or qualify only for, mortgages insured by the Federal Housing Administration. Such a shift in financing would still decrease the overall amount of risk borne by taxpayers, but the form of that risk would change slightly, which would have consequences for the federal budget.

Raising Fannie Mae's and Freddie Mac's guarantee fees would make loans insured by FHA more attractive to some borrowers. The new borrowers most likely to opt for FHA loans would be those with poor credit histories or small down payments. The large majority of borrowers who can make a 20 percent down payment—and thus avoid the cost of private mortgage insurance on GSEbacked loans—would be unlikely to choose FHA loans under any of the options for raising guarantee fees that CBO analyzed. Those borrowers would find private financing cheaper, even though CBO expects FHA's fees to decline under current policy, as the private sector recovers, toward the levels that existed before the financial crisis.

To determine which borrowers might shift from GSE- to FHA-backed mortgages, CBO compared how, under the options for raising guarantee fees, total fees (including premiums for private mortgage insurance) would differ for borrowers in different risk categories on the basis of their credit scores and down payments. That comparison suggests that if policymakers increased Fannie Mae's and Freddie Mac's guarantee fees by 10 basis points (and permanently extended the 10 basis-point increase in fees that is set to expire in 2021), about 5 percent of borrowers who might otherwise have had GSE-backed mortgages would have FHA-insured loans instead by 2024. That figure would be 10 percent if the GSEs' guarantee fees gradually increased by 50 basis points over the 2015– 2024 period. Even with the projected decline in FHA's fees, private financing would still be less expensive than FHA financing for most borrowers.

With changes in loan limits or a decline in the volume of new GSE guarantees as part of an auction process, CBO estimates that, initially, about

10 percent of the borrowers who were affected by those changes might switch to FHA financing because credit standards, including typical down payments, would remain high for loans above the conforming limit. As credit conditions in the private sector loosened over time, more borrowers would gain access to the private market. If that market recovered more quickly than CBO expects, fewer borrowers would shift to FHA. By contrast, if the availability of credit in the private market remained limited, the amount of FHA activity might rise substantially (assuming that appropriation actions were consistent with the increase in demand for FHA loans).

That analysis suggests that budgetary effects on FHA would be relatively modest under most of the options discussed in this Section but would be more significant under options that led to large fee increases or sizable reductions in loan limits. Those effects are discussed in more detail in the next Section.

SECTION 3. TRANSITIONS TO ALTERNATIVE STRUCTURES FOR THE SECONDARY MORTGAGE MARKET

Mechanisms such as higher guarantee fees, lower loan limits, risk-sharing requirements, and auctions of loan guarantees could be used in various ways to move the secondary mortgage market away from its current structure—dominance by two large government-sponsored enterprises in federal conservatorship—toward a new configuration. Selecting a new structure for the secondary market would involve making choices about the mix of public and private capital, the scope of any federal guarantees, and the role of the government during a financial crisis, among other considerations.

The Congressional Budget Office has analyzed potential transitions to four alternative structures for the secondary mortgage market:[1]

- A secondary market with a single, fully federal agency that would guarantee eligible mortgage-backed securities and leave taxpayers exposed to most of the credit risk on those securities;
- A hybrid public-private market in which the government and private investors would share the credit risk on eligible MBSs, with private investors bearing initial losses on those securities and the federal guarantee covering only catastrophic losses (an arrangement under which taxpayers would bear much of the risk of loss in a crisis and private investors would bear most of the risk in other periods);

- A secondary market in which the government plays a small role during normal times but acts as guarantor of last resort by fully guaranteeing most new mortgages during a financial crisis (at which time it would absorb all losses and gains on the securities based on those mortgages); and
- A largely private secondary market with no federal guarantees.

With any of those structures, the secondary market could continue to rely on securitization and other funding alternatives. The market could also retain roles for the Federal Housing Administration and other federal agencies that insure or guarantee mortgages, as well as for the Government National Mortgage Association, which offers securitization of mortgages for federal agencies. Private companies would continue to back mortgages that were ineligible for a federal guarantee, and the federal government could extend any explicit guarantee it might provide on qualified MBSs to covered bonds in order to promote more competition and greater diversity in mortgage funding.[2]

Each of those four market structures would have its own advantages and disadvantages in the following areas: ensuring a stable supply of financing for mortgages, protecting taxpayers from risk, providing incentives to control risk taking in the mortgage finance system, and making the allocation of credit risk between the government and the private sector transparent.[3] This Section discusses those advantages and disadvantages, as well as the key choices that policymakers would face in moving the market toward the new structures.

For each structure, CBO designed an illustrative transition path that involved choosing a specific set of options to attract private capital. The options selected for a particular path would move the secondary market toward a balance between public and private capital that is consistent with the market structure in question. The transition paths, which were designed to be implemented between 2015 and 2024, consist of hypothetical sets of policies that include various combinations of the mechanisms discussed in the previous Section—increases in guarantee fees, reductions in loan limits, sharing of credit risk, and auctions (see Table 3-1). In practice, policymakers could choose many other ways to use and combine those options, and they could alter the timetable to reach a given market structure sooner or later. Their choice of which options to use would be somewhat limited, however, by the structure that they hoped to transition to, as certain options are essential to bringing about a given structure.

CBO analyzed the effects of each of the hypothetical transition paths on federal subsidy costs, the volume of new loan guarantees by Fannie Mae and

Freddie Mac, the availability of credit, and other economic factors over the 2015–2024 period (see Table 3-2). The analysis reflects the assumptions that Fannie Mae and Freddie Mac would remain under federal control during that period and that the fair-value approach would be used to estimate the budgetary costs of subsidies for federal loan guarantees (as described in Section 1). Any new federal entities included in a particular market structure are assumed to begin operating in 2025, after the transition is completed. (Those entities would most likely be accounted for in the budget differently than are Fannie Mae and Freddie Mac because, unless the Congress specified otherwise, any new federal agency that provided an explicit federal guarantee under any of the options discussed here would be subject to the accounting method outlined in the Federal Credit Reform Act.) Whenever practical, CBO designed the transition paths so that the volume of new GSE guarantees at the end of the period would roughly match the desired federal share of the market under the new market structure. Consequently, in each of the illustrative paths, the market share for the two GSEs at the end of the transition period is assumed to be the starting point for any successor federal entities. Policymakers could, however, choose to aim for different market shares than those illustrated here.

Moving to a new structure for the secondary mortgage market would have implications for house prices, mortgage interest rates, and the activities of the Federal Housing Administration, among other things. New structures might also require decisions about what to do with the current operations and investment portfolios of Fannie Mae and Freddie Mac. Those other transition issues are discussed in Section 4. Any transition would probably also raise legal and regulatory issues that would take some time to resolve and are outside the scope of this analysis.

If changes such as those described in the transition paths were made in the next few years, care would need to be taken not to disrupt the housing and mortgage markets further. The sharp decline in house prices that occurred between 2006 and 2012 left many homeowners owing more on their mortgages than their homes are worth. As a result, foreclosure rates remain high, and obtaining a mortgage continues to be difficult for many people. A gradual, 5- to 10-year transition to a new market structure has a better chance of avoiding disruption in the housing and mortgage markets than does a more rapid shift. If, however, housing markets strengthened considerably, the risks associated with a faster transition would be lessened. One advantage of a faster transition is that it would reduce federal subsidies and the amount of mortgage credit risk borne by taxpayers more quickly than would a slower transition.

Transition to a Market with a Single, Fully Federal Agency

One approach for structuring the secondary mortgage market is to create a government agency to carry out the primary function now performed by Fannie Mae and Freddie Mac: providing explicit federal guarantees that promise timely payment of interest and principal on qualifying mortgages and MBSs that meet specified criteria. (The new agency's operations could share many features with the current activities of FHA and Ginnie Mae.) The cost of the federal agency could be covered, in whole or in part, by charging guarantee fees. Private entities would continue to provide financing for mortgages that were not eligible for a federal guarantee, but they would probably struggle to compete with the federal agency for most eligible mortgages unless government subsidies were eliminated.

Advantages and Disadvantages of the Structure

A federal guarantee agency could have some advantages over alternative market structures that rely on the private sector. For example, a government agency is more likely than are private investors to ensure a fairly steady flow of funds to the secondary mortgage market—both in normal times and during periods of financial stress—by minimizing uncertainty about the strength of federal guarantees. Moreover, most of the federal subsidies would probably flow to mortgage borrowers rather than to private financial institutions.

At the same time, however, creating a federal guarantee agency would strengthen government control of a large segment of the capital market, which may have negative consequences. Just how large that share would be depends on how the guarantees were priced and which mortgages were eligible for them. Such an arrangement may prove disadvantageous because the government has less incentive than do private parties to charge guarantee fees that cover costs (on a fair-value basis), so some borrowers would probably still be subsidized by taxpayers. Furthermore, taxpayers, rather than private financial institutions, would continue to bear much of the credit risk on guaranteed mortgages.[4] That risk-bearing arrangement might give mortgage originators and other financial intermediaries less incentive to control risk—a situation (known as moral hazard) that commonly arises with guarantees and insurance—than they would have under the alternative structures.

Table 3-1. Key Features of CBO's Illustrative Transition Paths to a New Structure for the Secondary Mortgage Market

	Current Policy (GSEs remain in conservatorship)	Transition to a Market With a Single, Fully Federal Agency	Transition to a Hybrid Public- Private Market	Transition to a Market With the Government as Guarantor of Last Resort	Transition to a Largely Private Secondary Market
Key Policy Changes	Not applicable	Establish a new federal agency	Increase sharing of credit risk	Hold auctions and raise loan limits	Raise fees and reduce loan limits
GSEs' Guarantee Feesa	Current fee schedule, including 10 basis-point drop in 2022, remains (Fees averaged 55 basis points in January 2014)	No changes	Raised by 10 basis points starting in 2015b	Set by auction; would probably rise by less than 10 basis points for most years	Raised by 20 basis points in 2015 and by 5 basis points annually from 2017 to 2022, for a total increase of 50 basis pointsb
GSEs' Loan Limitsc	$625,500 in high-cost areas, $417,000 elsewhere	Reduced to $417,000 in all areas	Reduced to $417,000 in all areas	Raised to $729,750 in all areas	Gradually reduced to zero
Sharing of Credit Riskd	Private mortgage insurance required for borrowers with less than 20 percent down payment	No changes	Investors take first losses from defaults of up to 10 percent of principal of new mortgages; GSEs guarantee against catastrophic losses	No changes	No changes

	Current Policy (GSEs remain in conservatorship)	Transition to a Market With a Single, Fully Federal Agency	Transition to a Hybrid Public- Private Market	Transition to a Market With the Government as Guarantor of Last Resort	Transition to a Largely Private Secondary Market
Auctions of New GSE Guarantees	None	None	None	First held in 2016; amount of new GSE guarantees auctioned off gradually reduced until GSEs cover only 10 percent of the market in 2024	None

Source: Congressional Budget Office.

Notes: A basis point is 0.01 percentage point.

GSEs = government-sponsored enterprises (specifically, Fannie Mae and Freddie Mac).

[a] In exchange for guaranteeing the timely payment of interest and principal on a mortgage, the GSEs receive fees from the lender (or the company servicing the lender's loans).

[b] In this transition path, the 10 basis-point increase in the GSEs' guarantee fees enacted in the Temporary Payroll Tax Cut Continuation Act of 2011, which is due to expire on October 1, 2021, is assumed to be extended permanently.

[c] Lawmakers have limited the size of mortgages that are eligible to be included in pools of loans guaranteed by the GSEs.

[d] In this case, sharing credit risk means that private parties absorb some amount of losses from loan defaults before the GSEs are required to do so.

Table 3-2. Probable Effects of CBO's Illustrative Transition Paths on Subsidy Costs, Loan Guarantees, the Availability of Credit, and Other Aspects of the Mortgage Market

	Transition to a Market With a Single, Fully Federal Agency	Transition to a Hybrid Public-Private Market	Transition to a Market With the Government as Guarantor of Last Resort	Transition to a Largely Private Secondary Market
Federal Subsidy Costs for the GSEs	Slight increases throughout the transition	Reduced to nearly zero by the end of the transition	Large declines throughout the transition	Reduced to zero by the end of the transition
Volume of New Loan Guarantees by the GSEs	Small declines throughout the transition	Moderate declines throughout the transition	Large declines by the end of the transition	Reduced to zero by the end of the transition
Availability of Credit During a Financial Crisis	Not affected	Less available	Not affected	Less Available
Other Aspects of the Mortgage Market	Federal government would maintain control of a large segment of the capital market	The GSEs' credit losses from defaults would drop significantly	Market mechanisms would ensure that guarantee fees reflect risk more fully	Financial institutions would have the strongest incentive to be prudent in their lending and securitizing

Source: Congressional Budget Office.

Notes: These effects are relative to CBO's projections of outcomes during the 2015–2024 period under current policy. GSEs = government-sponsored enterprises (specifically, Fannie Mae and Freddie Mac).

Key Policy Changes during the Transition

The transition from Fannie Mae and Freddie Mac to a fully federal agency could be accomplished without making any structural changes to guarantees, raising guarantee fees, or altering loan limits because no significant amounts of new private capital would be required. However, policymakers might opt to raise guarantee fees or lower the limits for conforming loans closer to the levels that existed before the financial crisis in order to reduce federal subsidies and modestly expand the private sector's role. Conversely, some policymakers might favor lowering guarantee fees to slow or stop the decline in the federal role that is projected to occur under current policy.

Illustrative Transition Path and Its Effects

In CBO's illustrative path to transition from the two GSEs in conservatorship to one fully federal agency, one or both of the GSEs would remain in place during the 2015–2024 period. By the end of that period, some of their operations would be folded into a new or existing federal agency, while others could be sold to the private sector (see the discussion at the end of Section 4). Although CBO assumed for consistency that the transition to any of the new market structures discussed in this Section would take place by 2024, a much shorter transition period might be sufficient to create a federal agency.

Under CBO's hypothetical path, policymakers would lower the GSEs' loan limits to $417,000 by 2016 but would keep guarantee fees at their current levels (those fees would still decline by 10 basis points beginning in 2022, as scheduled under current law). That path, CBO projects, would reduce Fannie Mae and Freddie Mac's total market share slightly, to about 40 percent by the end of the transition period, bringing the GSEs' share a bit closer to its average during the years before the financial crisis. The new federal agency would begin operating with that market share.

If CBO's transition path was followed, federal subsidy costs for the GSEs and interest rates on mortgages would probably be similar to those under current policy for most of the transition period. (However, if Fannie Mae and Freddie Mac were consolidated during the transition and issued a single set of MBSs, the liquidity of those securities would be enhanced, which could raise the price of MBSs and reduce interest rates to some extent. Currently, investors are willing to pay more for MBSs issued by Fannie Mae, which have become much more liquid than securities issued by Freddie Mac.)[5] The reduction in loan limits would cause the total volume of new guarantees made by the GSEs during that 10-year period to be $700 billion, or 5 percent, less than it would be under current policy, CBO projects (see Table 3-3 and Figure 3-1). Federal subsidies on GSE-backed mortgages over that period are projected to be only slightly higher (by less than $500 million) than under current law because Fannie Mae and Freddie Mac would probably lose their most profitable borrowers in the first few years of the transition. When the transition was completed, the interest rates paid by borrowers would depend on how the government chose to price its guarantees.

Transition to a Hybrid Public-Private Market

Another way to structure the secondary mortgage market is to decrease the federal government's role and increase the private sector's role while maintaining a combination of public and private financing. A key feature of such a hybrid system is that a federal guarantor and the private sector would share mortgage credit risk. For example, the government would help ensure a steady supply of mortgage financing by providing explicit guarantees on privately issued mortgages or MBSs that met certain qualifications. But private capital, and possibly private mortgage insurance, would absorb some credit losses before the government guarantee was invoked.

Proposals for a hybrid public-private structure vary widely, involving broader or narrower guarantees and more or less regulation of participants in the secondary market.[6] Some proposals call for the federal government to explicitly bear only catastrophic credit risks of the secondary market—an approach the government uses to reinsure commercial properties against the risk of terrorism.[7] (Catastrophic mortgage risks are those associated with severe downturns in the housing market.) Policy-makers could attempt to set federal guarantee fees at levels that would eliminate any subsidies. After the transition to the new structure was complete, Fannie Mae and Freddie Mac (or their successors) could be privatized and could compete with other private firms to securitize mortgages. Alternatively, the two GSEs could be liquidated, with some of their operating systems and nonfinancial assets sold to private firms. Other parts of their operations could be transformed into a new federal guarantor or merged into FHA or Ginnie Mae, which could provide guarantees against catastrophic losses.

Table 3-3. Effects of CBO's Illustrative Transition Paths on Projected Fair-Value Subsidy Costs and GSE Loan Guarantees, 2015 to 2024

(Billions of dollars)		
	Federal Subsidy Costs for the GSEs[a]	Amount of New Loan Guarantees by the GSEs
	CBO's Baseline	
Current Policy	19	13,500
	Effects of Illustrative Transition Paths to New Structures for the Secondary Mortgage Market	
Transition to a Market With a Single, Fully Federal Agency	*	-700
Transition to a Hybrid Public-Private Structure With Catastrophic Federal Guarantees	-10	-3,600
Transition to a Market With the Government as Guarantor of Last Resort	-11	-4,400
Transition to a Largely Private Secondary Market	-15	-10,200

Source: Congressional Budget Office.

Notes: For a description of the policy changes included in the illustrative transition paths, see Table 3 1. Those changes would begin in fiscal year 2015.

GSEs = government-sponsored enterprises (specifically, Fannie Mae and Freddie Mac); * = between zero and $500 million.

[a] Excludes potential effects on federal spending for the Federal Housing Administration (FHA) and the Government National Mortgage Association (Ginnie Mae). Spending on those agencies is set through annual appropriation acts and thus is classified as discretionary spending, whereas spending on Fannie Mae and Freddie Mac is not determined by appropriation acts and thus is classified as mandatory spending. In addition, FHA's annual commitments for new guarantees of single-family mortgages are subject to a limit set each year.

For this analysis, CBO assumed a transition to a structure under which any private financial institution that met certain regulatory criteria would be allowed to package and sell federally guaranteed MBSs backed by a pool of eligible mortgages.[8] Some liquidity might be lost by having several companies, rather than just the current two, issue federally backed MBSs unless those issues were standardized (as might be the case if a common securitization platform was created). However, the market would be less dependent on any one or two companies. (Financing for mortgages not eligible for federal backing would remain purely private, and the market for private-label MBSs with no government guarantees would continue.)

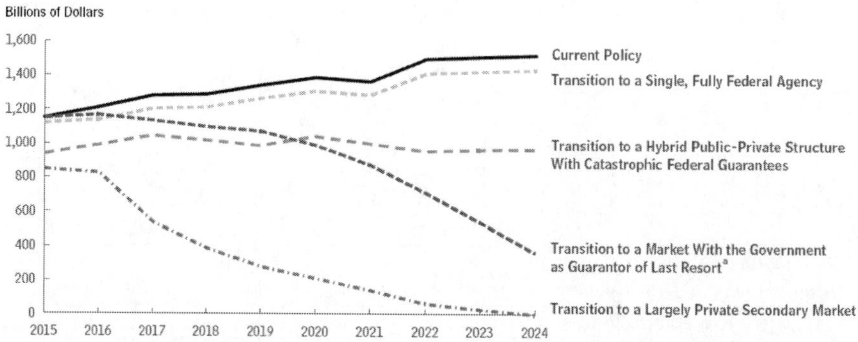

Notes: Under current policy, the increase in guarantee fees of 10 basis points (0.1 percentage point) that was authorized by the Temporary Payroll Tax Cut Continuation Act of 2011 is due to expire on October 1, 2021, which causes CBO's baseline projection of new guarantees to jump in 2022.

For a description of the policy changes included in the illustrative transition paths, see Table 3-1.

b. The transition to this market structure would not begin until 2016 to allow time for any implementation issues with auctions of Fannie Mae's and Freddie Mac's guarantees to be resolved.

Figure 3-1. Volume of New Loan Guarantees by Fannie Mae and Freddie Mac Under Illustrative Transition Paths to Different Market Structures.

CBO also assumed that the federal government would provide a secondary, or catastrophic, guarantee, which would be exercised only after private capital had borne an initial amount of losses. If that initial amount was set high enough, taxpayers would bear significant losses only during periods of financial stress. During a financial crisis, however, the secondary market would still be vulnerable to a retreat by private investors, which could make it difficult for homebuyers to obtain new mortgages. To reduce the chances of that happening, policymakers could lower the amount of credit risk that private investors are expected to hold for the duration of the crisis. Such a step would allow the government's guarantee to play a more stabilizing role in the secondary market.

Advantages and Disadvantages of the Structure

With private capital bearing initial credit losses, a hybrid approach would have the advantage of reducing costs and risks to taxpayers. Furthermore, private financial institutions would probably have stronger incentives to be prudent in their financing and their pricing of risk than the two GSEs have under conservatorship. Compared with establishing a fully federal agency, a hybrid public-private approach would alleviate concerns about putting a large portion of the capital market under government control. Compared with a predominantly private secondary market, a hybrid structure would probably improve the liquidity of the market, especially during times of financial stress.

Relying on explicit government guarantees of qualifying mortgages would, however, have some disadvantages. First, if competition remained limited—with only a few specialized firms participating in the secondary market— then any single firm's financial difficulties would pose a risk to the entire financial system. Second, experience with other federal insurance and credit programs suggests that the government would have trouble setting risk-sensitive guarantee fees and would most likely end up imposing some cost on taxpayers and exposing them to risk. (That concern would be lessened if market mechanisms such as auctions were used to set fees, provided that those mechanisms were efficiently designed.) Third, with a hybrid structure, mortgage financing might be less available during periods of market stress than it would be in a market with a fully federal agency or with the government acting as guarantor of last resort (as discussed below).

Key Policy Changes during the Transition

Policymakers would need to make some critical design choices about the structure of a public-private system. During the transition to that system, the main change from the status quo would be that Fannie Mae and Freddie Mac would share the credit risk on their mortgages with private investors. Policymakers might also want to reduce the number of mortgages that the entities guaranteed—by raising fees or lowering loan limits for the two GSEs, for example—so that private firms would capture a larger share of the market. Alternatively, policymakers could aim for a guarantee structure that exposed private investors to smaller initial losses and thus exposed the federal government to more frequent and larger losses. The various proposals made for a hybrid structure have called for a wide range of market shares for the federal government and different types of federal guarantees with different amounts of risk sharing. In addition, policy-makers could decide that a narrower or broader range of mortgages would be eligible for federal guarantees rather than retaining the current eligibility criteria for conforming mortgages.

Illustrative Transition Path and Its Effects

CBO created a transition path that combines higher guarantee fees and lower loan limits with risk-sharing provisions to allow Fannie Mae and Freddie Mac to shed the first 10 percent of the losses they now bear on individual mortgages. (If the market responded well to that change in the allocation of risk, the amount of risk shifted to the private sector could be increased as the transition progressed.) CBO estimates that the cost of the risk sharing—the amount of compensation that private investors and firms would require to assume that part of the two GSEs' risk—would be equivalent to about 14 basis points per year. Anticipating that policymakers would require the GSEs to absorb some of that cost but that they would pass most of it on to mortgage borrowers by raising guarantee fees, CBO based its estimates on an increase of 10 basis points in those fees. That increase, combined with a permanent extension of the 10 basis-point increase that is currently set to expire after 2021, would significantly reduce projected subsidy costs for new loan guarantees by Fannie Mae and Freddie Mac in most years. (Because policymakers could choose to adjust guarantee fees for changes in the price that private investors demanded for sharing risk, the actual increase in fees could be higher or lower.) Under the illustrative path, policymakers would also reduce the maximum size for conforming loans to $417,000 nationally by 2016, eliminating the special limit for high-cost areas.

Under a hybrid structure that incorporated federal guarantees against catastrophic losses, those guarantees would probably cover a much smaller share of the market than do Fannie Mae's and Freddie Mac's current guarantees. That is because, in CBO's judgment, private investors probably would not need a federal catastrophic guarantee to back the mortgages of most borrowers, at least outside periods of market stress. Borrowers with good credit scores and high down payments would very likely find private financing more attractive than federally backed loans. In the event of default, losses on those loans would most likely be relatively small and would not pose solvency risks to private firms. (Borrowers with low credit scores or low down payments present greater risks, however, and investors might want a federal guarantee against catastrophic losses to cover those loans.) The illustrative path would therefore reduce the GSEs' market share to about 27 percent by the 2024. If policymakers desired a higher or lower market share, they could use auctions to expand or limit the supply of guarantees.

If CBO's transition path was followed, Fannie Mae and Freddie Mac would issue about 27 percent fewer new loan guarantees between 2015 and 2024 than they would under current policy, primarily because of the higher fees associated with risk-sharing provisions. Those higher fees would raise interest rates on GSE-backed mortgages by 10 basis points for most of the period. Federal subsidy costs for Fannie Mae and Freddie Mac would be $10 billion lower over those 10 years than they would be under current policy (see Table 3-3 on page 38). (Those estimates reflect the assumption that the GSEs' financial activities would continue to be accounted for on a fair-value basis during the transition. If, instead, their transactions were estimated under a FCRA basis during the transition, then the estimate would be considerably different. See Box 3-1.) In addition, the GSEs' expected losses from mortgage defaults would be 35 percent lower than they would be under current law, CBO estimates, accounting for the possibility that private-sector entities might not be able to meet all of their risk-sharing obligations. By the end of the transition period, federal subsidies for Fannie Mae and Freddie Mac would be well below $500 million per year, and the interest rates that borrowers would face for new mortgages eligible for federal guarantees would be close to market rates (depending on how closely the government set its guarantee fees to those in the competitive market).

Policymakers could change the amount of risk that taxpayers were exposed to during the transition by adjusting both the amount of risk shifted to the private sector and the fees passed on to borrowers. For example, policy-makers could reduce taxpayers' risk by increasing the extent of risk sharing and by raising guarantee fees.

Transition to a Market with the Government as Guarantor of Last Resort

A third possibility for restructuring the secondary mortgage market is to establish a federal agency that would act as a final backstop, or guarantor of last resort, during periods of financial stress.[9] During normal times, private securitizers and banks would provide most of the funding for mortgages and bear most of the risks. However, the federal agency would maintain a continual presence in the market by guaranteeing a small share of all MBSs so that it would gain experience valuing a representative range of mortgages. That experience would help the government set its guarantee fees appropriately when, during a financial crisis, its presence expanded to cover most new MBSs. Such an expansion of the government's role could be tied to a significant drop in private mortgage lending or to some other triggering event. Once a crisis passed, the volume of new guarantees made by the federal agency would decline.

The new federal entity could be fashioned from Fannie Mae or Freddie Mac. Because it would usually operate on a much smaller scale than either of those GSEs, some of the two GSEs' operations could be sold (either liquidated or privatized). Alternatively, the Federal Housing Administration or Ginnie Mae could act as the guarantor of last resort.

Policymakers would use auctions, or some other competitive process, to set prices for federal guarantees and limit the number of those guarantees to a small share of the market—about 10 percent—in good times. During a crisis, however, the federal guarantor could set the size of auctions so as to cover a much higher percentage of MBSs. The size of the share of eligible loans the government chose to guarantee during a crisis could affect whether the bids in a competitive auction were high enough to eliminate most or all federal subsidies for loan guarantees. If, for example, the government faced pressure to guarantee all eligible mortgages, lenders would have little incentive to raise their bids, and the winning bids would probably include a subsidy (on a fair-value basis), assuming that the government set the minimum bid below the unsubsidized level. But if the size of the auctions remained a small fraction of the eligible market, firms would have to raise their bids to win guarantees. Those bids would probably reach fair-value levels and eliminate subsidies.

A market with the government as guarantor of last resort would differ from a hybrid public-private market with federal guarantees against catastrophic losses in two main ways. First, because the government would provide a full guarantee (at least during times of crisis) rather than a catastrophic guarantee, taxpayers would be exposed to all losses on newly guaranteed mortgages, without private firms' sharing any of the credit risk. Second, the federal guarantor would have little exposure to risk on loans guaranteed before a crisis because of its small market share in normal times. In some respects, that role resembles the one that FHA and Ginnie Mae played during the most recent financial crisis, except that the government would guarantee MBSs backed by a full range of mortgages rather than just mortgages with low down payments.

Box 3-1. Accounting for a New Federal Guarantor

The Federal Credit Reform Act of 1990 (FCRA) specifies the procedures to be used for recording the budgetary impact of most of the federal government's loan and loan guarantee programs. The FCRA accounting method is a present-value method for estimating subsidy costs that uses Treasury borrowing rates to discount expected future cash flows—that is, to translate future cash flows into a single, current-dollar estimate. Unless lawmakers specified an alternative budgetary treatment, the cost of the loan guarantees provided by a new federal guarantor would be accounted for in the budget in accordance with FCRA.

The Congressional Budget Office (CBO) does not currently account for the cost of the loan guarantees made by Fannie Mae and Freddie Mac on a FCRA basis; rather, it accounts for the activities of the two government-sponsored enterprises (GSEs) on a fair-value basis. In CBO's assessment, fair-value estimates provide a more comprehensive measure of cost than FCRA estimates because they incorporate the costs that private investors attach to financial risks by using market rates, rather than Treasury rates, to discount expected future cash flows. The costs of those risks are generally higher than the expected losses that are included in the FCRA estimates. CBO uses the same fair-value accounting methods to estimate the costs of administering the Troubled Asset Relief Program (as specified by the legislation that established the program) that it uses to account for the GSEs' activities (for which no guidance was provided in statute), but it uses FCRA accounting for other federal mortgage guarantee programs, such as those operated by the Federal Housing Administration.[1]

For estimates of the effects of policy alternatives in this report, CBO assumed that the cost of loan guarantees provided by Fannie Mae and Freddie Mac would continue to be accounted for on a fair-value basis (as they are in CBO's current estimates) and that no new federal guarantor would be in place until after the 10-year period that CBO typically uses for its cost estimates.

Lawmakers might, however, choose to have a new federal guarantor start operations during the transition or to account for Fannie Mae and Freddie Mac under FCRA accounting. Either of those actions would affect CBO's cost estimates of legislation to establish a new federal guarantor.

CBO's recent cost estimate for S. 1217, the Housing Finance Reform and Taxpayer Protection Act of 2014— a bill that would create a hybrid public-private structure with federal guarantees against catastrophic losses— illustrates the potential impact of different accounting measures for the federal guarantee on mortgage-backed securities (MBSs).[2] Under that bill, CBO projects, Fannie Mae and Freddie Mac would stop guaranteeing new MBSs at the end of 2019. Thereafter, a new entity, the Federal Mortgage Insurance Corporation (FMIC), would provide catastrophic federal guarantees for eligible MBSs in return for fees, but those guarantees would require federal payments only after private capital absorbed some of the losses. Because of the features of the bill, the government would take on less risk over the 2020–2024 period under FMIC guarantees than it would if the GSEs continued to operate as they do currently.

Under current law, CBO estimates, the mortgage guarantees offered by Fannie Mae and Freddie Mac over the 2020–2024 period will result in a positive subsidy cost of about $5 billion, calculated on a fair-value basis. Over that same period, CBO estimates, the guarantees offered by FMIC would result in savings to the federal government (that is, a negative subsidy cost) of about $47 billion, calculated using FCRA accounting. Those widely divergent budgetary effects are explained partly by the different terms of the guarantees offered by those entities. Most of the difference, however, stems from the two different accounting methods—FCRA and fairvalue—used to determine the costs of the guarantees that would be offered by FMIC or the GSEs. In its cost estimate for S. 1217, CBO provides the changes in mandatory spending on both a FCRA basis as required by law and a fair-value basis as additional information.

[1] For an analysis of the advantages and disadvantages of fair-value accounting, see testimony of Douglas W. Elmendorf, Director, Congressional Budget Office, before the House Committee on Financial Services, *Estimates of the Cost of the Credit Programs of the Export-Import Bank* (June 25, 2014), www.cbo.gov/publication/45468.

[2] Congressional Budget Office, cost estimate for S. 1217, the Housing Finance Reform and Taxpayer Protection Act of 2014 (September 5, 2014), www.cbo.gov/publication/ 45687.

Advantages and Disadvantages of the Structure

An advantage of limiting the government's role to guarantor of last resort is that it would mitigate a potentially critical shortcoming of the mortgage market: the inability of the private sector to provide a steady flow of credit during a financial crisis. Using auctions to determine guarantee fees would also help address the weak incentive that the government has traditionally had to price guarantees or set federal insurance premiums that reflect the full cost of those activities.

A major disadvantage of that approach, compared with risk sharing, is that the government would have to pay the full amount of any losses for all of the guarantees assumed during a crisis. Thus, taxpayers could be exposed to most of the credit risk from mortgages originated in a crisis. Moreover, how adroit a federal entity would be in responding to a crisis and then letting its role diminish is uncertain.

Key Policy Changes during the Transition

Auctions, or some other competitive process, would be a key component of the government's transition to being the guarantor of last resort. During that transition, policy- makers could require Fannie Mae and Freddie Mac to begin experimenting with auctions in order to gain the experience with risk-based pricing that would be necessary for guaranteeing a representative sample of mortgages. (If, instead of adjusting guarantee fees for the riskiness of borrowers, the two GSEs raised fees uniformly for all borrowers, they would gradually lose their lowest-risk borrowers to the private sector.) Policymakers could also raise Fannie Mae's and Freddie Mac's loan limits to expand the pool of borrowers eligible for federal guarantees, which would give the GSEs experience pricing a broader range of mortgages.

If only a full federal guarantee can ensure stability in a crisis—which is a matter of contention—sharing risk with private investors during periods of financial stress would undermine that stability. Risk sharing could, however, be a viable option in normal times.

Illustrative Transition Path and Its Effects

For this analysis, CBO selected a transition path under which policymakers would use auctions to gradually reduce Fannie Mae and Freddie Mac's total market share to about 10 percent by 2024—a target that is consistent with minimizing the government's role in the secondary market during normal periods. The start of the transition would be delayed until 2016 to allow more time to test auctions before getting them up and running on a large scale. For simplicity, CBO assumed that the volume of guarantees sold in the auctions would be large initially but would then shrink steadily. Under the path, policy-makers would raise the limit on conforming loans to $729,750 nationwide in 2016. (Alternatively, regulators could begin by having Fannie Mae and Freddie Mac auction off guarantees on mortgages between $417,000 and $729,750 as early as 2015.)

With auctions limiting access to GSE-backed mortgages, the volume of new guarantees by Fannie Mae and Freddie Mac during the 2015–2024 period would be about 33 percent lower under the illustrative path than it would be under current policy, CBO projects. (However, if a financial crisis occurred during the transition to this market structure, Fannie Mae and Freddie Mac would see a large increase in their activity.) If the auctions were well designed, federal subsidy costs for new guarantees over that period would be reduced by $11 billion (see Table 3-3 on page 38). By 2024, the GSEs' new guarantees would amount to less than $400 billion a year, and federal subsidies would be nearly eliminated. After the transition was completed, most mortgage borrowers would pay market interest rates during normal times, when the federal guarantor of last resort played a small role in the market. Interest rates might, however, fall below market levels during times of financial crises, when the guarantor played a larger role.

How far guarantee fees would rise and subsidies would fall in normal times with this market structure would depend on how well the bidding process worked. CBO expects that guarantee fees would probably be up to 5 basis points higher than under current policy in most years, which would increase interest rates on GSE-backed mortgages by a similar amount. Federal subsidies would not be completely eliminated, CBO projects, because mortgage originators would have more information about the quality of their loans than would Fannie Mae and Freddie Mac. (Despite the required disclosures about the composition of loan pools, all risk factors on a loan would probably still not be fully apparent.) The pools of eligible mortgages that the GSEs guaranteed might therefore be of lower-than-expected quality (at least initially).

Furthermore, if the GSEs sold a relatively large number of guarantees (as they would need to do in the early years of the transition to avoid shrinking the federal presence too quickly), firms might be deterred from bidding at a level that involved no subsidy. Firms might also bid less aggressively if there were only a small number of competitors. It is possible, however, that bids could be high enough in all of those cases to eliminate subsidies.

Transition to a Largely Private Secondary Market

At the opposite end of the spectrum from a secondary market dominated by the government is a market that is left mainly to the private sector, with no explicit federal guarantees of MBSs.[10] In this analysis, CBO assumes that FHA, the Department of Veterans Affairs, and the Rural Housing Service, whose loans are all securitized by Ginnie Mae, would continue to guarantee mortgages. To achieve a market structure without other direct federal involvement, lawmakers could gradually phase out the operations of Fannie Mae and Freddie Mac, or they could sell the federal stake in the two GSEs' assets to private investors. Either way, the market for mortgage-backed securities would ultimately be dominated by private firms—just as are the markets for securities backed by other types of assets (the markets for automobile, student, commercial real estate, and credit card loans, for example).

In times of severe distress, the government could still step in to ensure the availability of financing in the mortgage market. For instance, it could make FHA guarantees available to more borrowers, or it could buy private-label MBSs. Expanding the activities of federal agencies in those circumstances, however, would generally require Congressional action.

Advantages and Disadvantages of the Structure

Of the market structures that CBO analyzed, privatization would probably provide the strongest incentive for financial institutions to be prudent in their lending and securitizing because private investors, rather than taxpayers, would bear all losses. (On the other hand, the enormous losses that have occurred in recent years on private-label subprime mortgages, which are not federally guaranteed, offer a clear reminder that private markets are not immune to aggressive risk taking.) Furthermore, by increasing competition in the secondary market, a privatization approach would reduce the market's reliance on the viability of any single firm. A private market may also be best positioned to allocate the credit risks and interest rate risks of mortgages efficiently, and it would be more innovative than a secondary market with a fully federal agency playing a prominent role. The lack of a federal backstop might encourage financial institutions and their regulators to seek out other forms of stable, long-term financing for mortgages, such as covered bonds (which many European banks use to fund the mortgages they hold), as an alternative to securitization.[11]

Full privatization could have several drawbacks, however, including the possibility that a private secondary market might be significantly less liquid than a market with some federal backing, especially during periods of acute financial stress. For example, in the most recent crisis, private securitization virtually ceased, and issuance of privately financed mortgages severely contracted, leaving less than 10 percent of new mortgage credit privately backed in 2009. That sharp contraction in the availability of private mortgage credit hurt economic growth and probably contributed to lower house prices, despite a significant increase in federally guaranteed credit.

In addition, committing to a policy of nonintervention in the mortgage market might not prove credible if the availability of mortgage credit is disrupted in the future. If the private firms operating in the secondary market were seen as critical to the functioning of the mortgage finance system, investors might again treat them as implicitly guaranteed by the federal government. That perception could cause investors in the firms' securities to demand less compensation for risk than they would otherwise, which in turn could encourage the firms to take on too much risk, thus weakening the financial system.

Implicit federal guarantees would also reduce transparency. The costs and risks of those guarantees to taxpayers would not appear in the federal budget, so policymakers would have difficulty assessing them.

Key Policy Changes during the Transition

Policymakers could begin to attract private capital to the secondary mortgage market by raising Fannie Mae's and Freddie Mac's guarantee fees and lowering their loan limits. Those changes could continue until the GSEs' share of the market for new mortgage guarantees reached zero. Policymakers could also expand risk-sharing opportunities beyond those currently envisioned by regulators, although such a change would not be essential for privatization.

Illustrative Transition Path and Its Effects

CBO analyzed a transition path in which policymakers would gradually raise guarantee fees by 50 basis points over the 2015–2024 period—starting with a 20 basis-point increase in 2015, no change in 2016, and then 5 basis-point increases in each of the following six years—and gradually reduce Fannie Mae's and Freddie Mac's loan limits to zero by 2024. Those policy changes would cause the volume of new GSE guarantees during that period to be 75 percent lower than it would be under current policy, CBO estimates. In the early years of the transition, the higher fees for GSE backing would contribute to that decline by giving borrowers an incentive to find cheaper private financing. Later in the period, the decrease in the GSEs' loan limits would reduce borrowers' alternatives.

That illustrative path would reduce projected subsidy costs for new GSE guarantees made during the 2015– 2024 period by $15 billion (see Table 3-3 on page 38). Moreover, the rise in guarantee fees would cause interest rates on GSE-backed mortgages to increase steadily during that period until they reached market rates, closing the spread between rates on privately backed and federally backed mortgages.

Under that illustrative path, no new guarantees by Fannie Mae or Freddie Mac would be made—and therefore no further subsidy costs would be incurred—after 2023, thus completing the transition to a fully private market for new mortgages. Thereafter, interest rates on new mortgages would remain at market levels.

SECTION 4. OTHER TRANSITION ISSUES

Atransition to any of the new structures for the secondary mortgage market that are discussed in Section 3 would affect mortgage borrowers, the housing market, and the Federal Housing Administration. Those effects would vary depending on the magnitude of the decline in federal subsidies, the degree of the market's reliance on the private sector, and the speed of the transition. As long as the transition was gradual, the impact on mortgage interest rates and house prices should be moderate—probably smaller than the fluctuations in interest rates and house prices that occur in most years. In addition, to reduce the possibility of disruptions in the availability of credit, policymakers could make the pace of the transition contingent on how the private sector responded.

Although Fannie Mae and Freddie Mac would continue to guarantee mortgage-backed securities throughout each of the transitions analyzed in this report, moving from a market so reliant on those two government-sponsored enterprises to any new structure would involve making decisions about what to do with their operating assets as well as their existing investment portfolios and guarantee obligations. Specifically, policymakers would need to decide whether the two GSEs' operating assets would be kept for use by a federal agency or auctioned off to private firms, and they would also need to decide whether the GSEs' sizable portfolios and obligations would be retained by the government or transferred to private investors.

Effects of the Transitions on Mortgage Borrowers and the Housing Market

Under any of the transitions that CBO examined, the agency expects that most borrowers would still be able to take out 30-year fixed rate mortgages. During a transition, reducing subsidies for the GSEs' loan guarantees would reduce the availability of mortgage credit, raise the interest rates that borrowers pay on new mortgages, and decrease house prices (see Table 4-1). Those effects would probably be mitigated by at least two factors. First, CBO projects that private financing of mortgages will gradually rise over the course of any of the 10-year transitions as the housing market recovers and conditions in financial markets normalize. Second, the GSEs' fees under current policy will be very close to those that a private guarantor would charge by 2024, CBO anticipates, which means that most borrowers who took out mortgages at the end of a transition would receive terms that were roughly comparable to those in the baseline.

Depending on the transition, the increase in interest rates would probably range between 5 and 60 basis points for most borrowers, CBO estimates, and as a result, house prices might be as much as a 2.5 percent lower than they would be under current policy. In addition, the increase in interest rates would reduce investment in housing, but because the increase is expected to be less than 60 basis points for most borrowers—and significantly less for many—the reduction in housing investment relative to the baseline would probably be modest. Generally speaking, the magnitude of each of those effects would be largest in the transition to a mainly private market and smallest in the transition to a market with a fully federal agency. During any transition, lawmakers might also want to provide some flexibility to regulators to respond to unexpected changes in market conditions in order to lessen the possibility of disruptions in mortgage availability.

Although not included in this report, other issues that policymakers would have to address before a transition are the extent of the GSEs' involvement in the smaller secondary market for mortgages on multifamily properties and their role in promoting housing for low-income people.

Table 4-1. Probable Effects of CBO's Illustrative Transition Paths on the Mortgage and Housing Markets

	Transition to a Market With a Single, Fully Federal Agency	Transition to a Hybrid Public-Private Market	Transition to a Market With the Government as Guarantor of Last Resort	Transition to a Largely Private Secondary Market
Availability of 30-Year Fixed Rate Mortgages	Not affected	Not affected	Widely available when the securitization market is liquid; probably disrupted when the market is frozen	Widely available when the securitization market is liquid; probably disrupted when the market is frozen
Interest Rates for Most Borrowers of GSE-Backed Mortgages	Not affected (Slight increases throughout the transition on loans without GSE backing)	Small increases throughout the transition	Small increases throughout the transition (Larger increases on loans without GSE backing)	Moderate increases by the end of the transition (Larger increases throughout the transition period on loans without GSE backing)
House Prices	Not noticeably affected	Slightly lower throughout the transition	Slightly lower by the end of the transition	Slightly lower by the end of the transition
Investment in Housing	Underpricing of risk would persist, continuing the current overallocation of capital toward housing	Underpricing of risk would decrease, reducing the allocation of capital toward housing	Underpricing of risk would decrease, reducing the allocation of capital toward housing	Underpricing of risk would decrease, reducing the allocation of capital toward housing
Volume of Loans Insured by FHA	Small increases throughout the transition	Moderate increases throughout the transition	Moderate increases throughout the transition	Large increases by the end of the transition

Source: Congressional Budget Office.

Notes: These effects are relative to CBO's projections of outcomes during the 2015–2024 period under current policy.

GSEs = government-sponsored enterprises (specifically, Fannie Mae and Freddie Mac); FHA = Federal Housing Administration.

Availability of 30-Year Fixed Rate Mortgages

During a transition, banks would probably continue to make 30-year fixed rate mortgages widely available as long as the securitization market was large and liquid, whether or not that market had government backing.[1] Therefore, such mortgages would remain prevalent in either a market with a fully federal guarantee agency or a hybrid public-private market. However, in a market in which the government acted only as guarantor of last resort or in one that was largely private, the availability of long-term fixed rate mortgages would depend on the state of private securitization markets. In the past, when the liquidity of private-label MBSs was strong, 30-year fixed rate mortgages were widely available in the jumbo market. But when private securitization froze during the financial crisis, originations of fixed rate jumbo mortgages dropped disproportionately.

Long-term fixed rate mortgages offer borrowers who plan to stay in their current residences for many years a predictable payment schedule and the opportunity to refinance if interest rates fall. Those same features expose banks and investors (including those holding MBSs guaranteed by Fannie Mae and Freddie Mac) to considerable risk and make such mortgages difficult to evaluate and price: If interest rates fall unexpectedly, borrowers tend to pay off their loans ahead of schedule in order to refinance at lower rates. Banks are therefore more likely to originate 30-year fixed rate mortgages when those loans can be securitized, which removes the credit, interest rate, and prepayment risks from their balance sheets. As a result, if securitization opportunities declined under a transition either to a structure in which the government acts as guarantor of last resort or to a largely private secondary market, 30-year fixed rate mortgages would be likely to carry higher interest rates and be more susceptible to disruptions in supply than mortgages that are easier for investors to evaluate and price.

Unlike European borrowers, who tend to favor adjustable rate mortgages, U.S. borrowers have generally shown a strong preference for the predictable payment schedules of 30-year fixed rate mortgages and have therefore been willing to pay somewhat higher interest rates for such loans than they would have had to pay for adjustable rate mortgages.[2] That preference may have been influenced by government policy, which, by making the secondary market more liquid, has tended to subsidize 30-year fixed rate loans more than other types of mortgages. (Because banks and thrifts can more readily hold adjustable rate mortgages than fixed rate mortgages on their balance sheets, rates on adjustable rate mortgages are less affected by the added market liquidity that comes from the GSEs' securitization of mortgages.) Some borrowers who take out fixed rate loans but who anticipate moving or refinancing might actually be better off with an adjustable rate mortgage than with a fixed rate mortgage because they pay a premium for the long-term predictability of that fixed rate.

Interest Rates

Each of the illustrative transition paths described in Section 3 would leave at least some categories of borrowers facing higher interest rates during the transitions than they would face under current policy.[3] The rate increases would vary across borrowers and would depend on what type of transition path was chosen.

The increase in interest rates for a given borrower would depend on the type of mortgage financing sought by the borrower and on his or her creditworthiness:

- Borrowers who took out mortgages guaranteed by the two GSEs would generally face rates that were comparable to those they would pay under current policy or were slightly higher because of increases in guarantee fees.
- Low-risk borrowers who chose to take out privately backed mortgages because increases in guarantee fees raised the cost of GSE-backed loans above the cost of loans offered in the private market would generally face only slightly higher mortgage rates during a transition than they would with GSE-backed mortgages under current policy. The increase in the rates they paid would be small because those borrowers receive very small subsidies under current policy.
- Average borrowers who relied on privately guaranteed mortgages—whether because their mortgages exceeded the GSEs' reduced loan limits or because they were deterred by the GSEs' higher guarantee fees—would experience rate increases that were greater than those experienced by low-risk borrowers but still moderate.
- Less creditworthy borrowers who lost access to GSEbacked financing during a transition would probably fare significantly worse than they would under current policy because the GSEs' guarantees currently provide them with significant subsidies. Those high-risk borrowers would probably also see a decrease in the availability of mortgages as private firms would have somewhat tighter lending standards than the two GSEs—requiring higher down payments, for example—but many of those borrowers could turn to FHA loans instead.

The effects on interest rates would also depend on the type of transition policymakers chose to make:

- In a transition to a market with a single, fully federal agency, borrowers who took out GSE-backed mortgages would face mortgage rates comparable to those they would pay on GSE-backed mortgages under current policy. Borrowers who were forced into private financing by policymakers' lowering of loan limits would pay higher rates than they would under current policy, but that increase would be only slight because those borrowers tend to be low risk and therefore receive the smallest subsidies from the GSEs under current policy.
- In a transition to a hybrid public-private market, borrowers who took out mortgages backed by the GSEs would face rates that were no more than 20 basis points higher than they would be under current policy. For borrowers who were forced into private financing by the lowering of loan limits, the increase in rates relative to those under current policy would be slight, for the reason just described.
- In a transition to a market in which the government acts as guarantor of last resort, borrowers who took out mortgages backed by the GSEs would face rates that were about 5 basis points higher than they would be under current policy, CBO estimates. Because auctions of GSE-backed guarantees would limit their supply, by the end of the transition most borrowers would rely on private financing and would therefore face higher rates. Depending on market conditions, those increases would, according to CBO's estimates, range from 10 basis points to 60 basis points for most borrowers, with higher-risk borrowers facing the largest increases.
- In a transition to a largely private market, borrowers who took out GSE-backed loans early in the transition would pay interest rates that were 20 basis points higher than they would pay under current policy. That differential would continue to increase, so by 2024, borrowers who took out federally backed mortgages would face rates that were 60 basis points higher than they would be under current policy. However, most borrowers would switch to private financing during the transition and would face rates between 10 basis points and 60 basis points higher than under current policy, CBO estimates, with higher-risk borrowers facing the largest increases.

Holding all else equal, those increases in interest rates would raise monthly mortgage payments, increasing the potential for borrowers to default on their loans, reducing the demand for houses, and leaving borrowers with less income to cover other expenses.[4] The effects would, however, tend to be modest for borrowers who continued to obtain GSE-backed loans because the expected interest rate increases for those borrowers are fairly small. For example, a 10 basis-point increase in guarantee fees—and thus in interest rates—would raise the monthly payment on a $200,000 30-year fixed rate mortgage by less than $15. By contrast, borrowers who turned to private financing would experience more significant rate increases and therefore larger increases in monthly payments. A 30 basis-point increase, for example, would raise the monthly payment on a $200,000 mortgage by about $40.

Even those larger increases would still be smaller than the fluctuations in market interest rates that occur in most years. For example, rates on conforming 30-year fixed rate mortgages rose from less than 3.5 percent in January 2013 to 4.5 percent in July of that year, or more than 100 basis points. Mortgage rates moved a little less during the first 11 months of 2014, when they stayed between 3.9 percent and 4.5 percent, a range of 60 basis points.

Some other analysts expect that a transition to a largely private market could cause mortgage interest rates for the average borrower to rise by 100 basis points or more, which is a significantly larger increase than CBO projects.[5] Those analysts argue that attracting more private capital to mortgage markets would require significantly higher rates of return on MBSs and mortgages than private investors or banks currently receive, and that to improve those returns, banks would incorporate higher risk premiums into the interest rates they charged borrowers. But if rates rose as significantly as some analysts predict, borrowers would be more likely to switch from fixed rate mortgages to lower-cost adjustable rate mortgages, whose rates are less affected by conditions in the securitization markets.

Moreover, it is also possible that transition paths that led to greater involvement of the private sector in the secondary mortgage market might make the market for private-label MBSs more liquid than CBO anticipates. If that was the case, the increases in interest rates would be less than CBO expects.

House Prices

Increases in mortgage interest rates that resulted from the transitions analyzed in this report would cause house prices to increase at a slower rate than they would under current policy, but in CBO's view, it is unlikely that they would lead to outright declines in house prices. Analysts have estimated that a 1 percentage-point increase in real rates could reduce house prices by anywhere from 1 percent to 8 percent of what they would be under current policy. On the basis of those estimates, CBO projects that the transitions would have the following effects:

- In a transition to a market with a single, fully federal agency, house prices would show no noticeable effects.
- In a transition to a hybrid public-private market, house prices would be lower than they would be under current policy by no more than 1 percent during most of the transition and by as much as 2 percent at the end of the transition.
- In a transition to a market in which the government acts as guarantor of last resort, house prices would probably be affected more significantly than they would be under the preceding two transitions. If interest rates for the average borrower increased by about 30 basis points, house prices could be as much as 2.5 percent lower than under current policy.
- In a transition to a largely private market, house prices would be affected to about the same degree as in a transition to a market in which the government acts as guarantor of last resort. If interest rates for the average borrower increased by about 30 basis points, house prices could be as much as 2.5 percent lower than under current policy. However, in the unlikely event that a crisis occurred during the transition, the effects could be much greater.

A number of other factors are likely to affect house prices more significantly than the changes in interest rates brought about by the transition paths discussed in this report, especially in the current environment. Those factors include changes in lending standards, the inventory of unsold homes, the volume of foreclosures and other distressed sales, the supply of new housing, the growth of income, unemployment rates, and expectations about future changes in house prices.[6] Potential changes in tax provisions could also have a significant impact on house prices.[7]

Investment in Housing

Federal subsidies for mortgage guarantees lead to the underpricing of mortgage risk and therefore distort the allocation of capital in the economy, shifting some investment toward housing that might otherwise go to business equipment and structures that increase the productivity of workers. Some advocates for those subsidies maintain that home ownership gives households a greater stake in their communities, making those communities more stable. However, the slightly below-market guarantee fees that the GSEs now charge do little to boost rates of home ownership because down payment requirements are a bigger barrier to home ownership than the size of monthly mortgage payments and because the subsidized guarantee fees are probably largely capitalized in house prices and thus do not make housing much more affordable for new purchasers.[8]

Of the four transitions that CBO analyzed, the transitions to a fully private market or to a market with the government as guarantor of last resort would bring about the largest reductions in federal subsidies and therefore the greatest shifts of capital away from housing and to other investments. However, because the increases in interest rates under even those transitions are expected to be moderate, the reductions in housing investment relative to the baseline would probably be modest. A transition to a market with a fully federal agency playing a prominent role would have little effect on the allocation of capital because federal subsidies would be little changed. And a transition to a hybrid public-private structure would cause smaller reductions in housing investment than would a transition to either a structure under which the government acted as guarantor of last resort or to a fully private market.

Potential Market Disruptions during the Transition to a New Structure

If a transition to a new structure for mortgage finance led to an unexpected contraction of mortgage availability or to a sharp spike in mortgage rates, the economic costs could be high. A key concern about transitioning to a largely private secondary market is that it might fail to ensure a stable supply of mortgage credit during periods of financial stress. During such occasions, uncertainty about the solvency of private guarantors could erode confidence in private credit guarantees, causing mortgage interest rates to rise sharply. The adverse effects of such a rise on the housing market would deepen economic distress.

One approach to preventing such an outcome would be to make the pace of the transition conditional on changes in the availability of private mortgage credit.[9] For example, instead of reducing Fannie Mae's and Freddie Mac's loan limits all at once or by preset amounts each year, lawmakers could specify a flexible reduction schedule that would give regulators the discretion to respond to unexpected changes in mortgage credit conditions: Loan limits could be lowered more quickly if credit was widely available and more slowly if credit was more limited. Such an approach would require regulators to construct a metric to measure changes in credit conditions or to use an existing private-sector one.[10] Private-sector indicators of mortgage credit availability are regularly updated and verifiable, so measurement issues should not be a large hurdle to using this approach.

As a second alternative to adopting a fixed schedule, policymakers could specify a target for the GSEs' market share and allow regulators to adjust guarantee fees and loan limits as needed to hit the target. Gradual increases in fees and decreases in limits could be halted once the GSEs' market share reached the target or even reversed if that share dipped below the target. Conversely, if the GSEs' market share fell too slowly, the pace of the increases in fees and decreases in limits could be accelerated. Although that approach would provide more stable mortgage finance than a fixed schedule of changes in guarantee fees and loan limits, it would probably be less effective in reducing potential disruptions than making the pace of the transition conditional on the availability of private credit. During periods of market disruptions, maintaining the availability of mortgage credit would probably require the GSEs' role to be larger, which might not be possible with a targeted market share.

CBO did not estimate the budgetary effects of such approaches, referred to as circuit breakers. Those approaches might produce smaller or larger budgetary savings than would a fixed transition path, depending on whether the pace of changes slowed down or sped up.

Effects of the Transitions on the Federal Housing Administration

All of the illustrative transition paths that CBO examined would reduce the amount of credit risk backed by the government through the GSEs or successor agencies. The government's overall exposure to risk would not decline by a commensurate amount, however, because some of the borrowers who would have GSE-backed mortgages under current policy would turn to FHA-insured single-family loans instead. That increase in the volume of FHA guarantees would have budgetary effects.

Increases in FHA Guarantees

Under a transition to a new market structure, some borrowers would shift from mortgages financed by Fannie Mae and Freddie Mac to mortgages guaranteed by FHA, whether because of the reduced availability of GSE financing or because of higher GSE fees. The borrowers most likely to secure FHA-backed mortgages rather than privately backed mortgages would be the riskiest ones— those who had relatively low credit scores or could not meet the down payment standards of the private market. That pattern would occur because borrowers who could make a down payment of 20 percent, or in many cases even 10 percent, would have little incentive to consider switching to FHA-backed mortgages under the transition paths (barring an unexpected shock to the mortgage market). Unlike fees in the private market, FHA's fees do not vary significantly with the size of borrowers' down payments and do not vary at all with borrowers' credit scores. As a result, in CBO's assessment, the fees that FHA charges less risky borrowers will be higher than those charged by Fannie Mae, Freddie Mac, and private mortgage insurers under current policy or under any of the illustrative transition paths, even after accounting for the increases in the GSEs' fees that are included in some of them.

Under current policy, FHA's loan volume for single-family mortgages over the 2015–2024 period will be more than $2.2 trillion, according to CBO's April 2014 projections. During the transition to a market with a single, fully federal agency, FHA's loan volume for that period would increase by roughly $60 billion as borrowers shifted from GSE financing, CBO estimates.[11] That increase would be a small share of the projected volume under current policy because only a small share of borrowers would be affected by the lower GSE loan limits during the transition. During a transition to a hybrid public-private market or to a market with the government acting as guarantor of last resort, CBO estimates that the increase in FHA's loan volume over the 2015– 2024 period would be roughly $400 billion. And during a transition to a largely private market, the increase in FHA's loan volume over the coming decade would be about $900 billion. Those increases would range from about 2 percent to 40 percent of the size of FHA's insurance program under current policy.

The Budgetary Effects of Additional FHA Guarantees on a FCRA Basis

Estimates of the government's subsidy costs for FHA guarantees, like those for most other federal credit programs, are reported in accordance with the procedures specified in the Federal Credit Reform Act, which require discounting expected cash flows at Treasury rates. Under those procedures, FHA's single-family guarantees are recorded in the budget with a negative subsidy cost. In other words, the present value of the payments that the government will receive over the lifetime of the loans that FHA will insure in the next 10 years is projected to be greater than the present value of the payments that the government will make for defaults on those loans. If legislators approved, and borrowers sought, a larger amount of loan guarantees by FHA, those additional loans would generate additional estimated budgetary savings.

Federal credit generally appears to be less costly when reported on a FCRA basis than it does on a fair-value basis, so under current budgetary procedures, proposals that replaced GSE guarantees (accounted for at fair value) with FHA guarantees (accounted for under FCRA) would result in estimates of budgetary savings that are an artifact of switching the accounting treatment of those guarantees. Under the path to a market with a single, fully federal agency, those savings would amount to an additional $2 billion, CBO estimates, on top of the estimated $63 billion in savings from FHA's single-family guarantees under current policy. Under the paths that focus on attracting more private capital, the added savings during that period would range from $8 billion (under a transition to a market with the government acting as guarantor of last resort) to $22 billion (under a transition to a largely private market).

The estimates reflect CBO's judgment that FHA's insurance fees will decline over time. Under current law, FHA has some flexibility to adjust fees, but the process for setting loan limits is set by statute. Because current fees are higher than is necessary to build FHA's reserves back up to the level required by law, CBO anticipates that FHA will lower those fees.[12] Some legislative proposals would, however, raise those fees above the levels projected in CBO's baseline (though still below current levels), reduce FHA's loan limits in high-cost areas, and impose income restrictions for borrowers who were not first-time homebuyers.[13] If enacted, those changes would lessen the shift in guarantees from Fannie Mae and Freddie Mac to FHA under the transitions analyzed in this report, which reflects the assumption that FHA would continue to operate under current policy.

The Budgetary Effects of Additional FHA Guarantees on a Fair-Value Basis

On a fair-value basis, CBO estimates that FHA's single-family loan guarantees typically have a positive subsidy cost, meaning that the amount that the government would need to pay private entities to assume those loan guarantee receipts and obligations is positive.[14] Thus, if fair-value accounting was used for FHA, the shift in loan guarantees from Fannie Mae and Freddie

Mac to that agency would boost subsidy costs for FHA (under an assumption that appropriations would be consistent with the expected increase in demand for FHA guarantees) and reduce the savings shown in the illustrative transition paths.

Under current policy, those subsidies will have a cost of $27 billion over the 2015–2024 period on a fair-value basis, CBO projects. Over that same period, the transition to a market with a fully federal agency in place of the two GSEs would increase fair-value subsidy costs for FHA by about $1 billion. The transition paths that brought in more private capital would increase FHA subsidies over 10 years by between $6 billion (under a transition to either a hybrid market or to a market with the government acting as guarantor of last resort) and $14 billion (under a transition to a largely private market).

Thus, under FCRA accounting, an increase in the volume of FHA guarantees generates savings, but under fair-value accounting, that increase would result in net costs. FCRA estimates may be more useful than fair-value estimates in projecting the average budgetary effects of programs that provide credit assistance, but projecting such effects is not the only, or necessarily even the primary, purpose of estimates of the cost of changes in federal programs. Cost estimates are tools that policy-makers can use to make trade-offs between different policies that work toward a particular policy goal. By taking into account how the public assesses financial risks as expressed through market prices, fair-value estimates may be more useful than FCRA estimates in helping policy-makers understand trade-offs between policies that involve such risks.

Under a transition to a market with a fully federal agency, the difference in the two measures is relatively small— about $2 billion. The differences are much more significant in transitions to other market structures, where the effects on the volume of FHA guarantees would be greater. For example, a transition to a largely private market would show savings for FHA of $22 billion under FCRA but a cost of $14 billion under fair-value accounting—a difference of $36 billion.

Effects of the Transitions on Fannie Mae's and Freddie Mac's Existing Operations

Any transition to a new secondary mortgage market structure would require decisions about how to restructure the two GSEs as institutions and how to manage their existing assets and liabilities. Those decisions would depend in part on the long-term role that policymakers wanted the government to play.

Under CBO's fair-value accounting for the GSEs, any sales of Fannie Mae's and Freddie Mac's assets that occurred at market prices in orderly transactions would be considered an exchange of an asset for a cash amount of equal value—so the only budgetary costs would be the costs involved in conducting the transactions. Under other accounting treatments, however, the budgetary costs of selling portfolio holdings or of paying private parties to take over the GSEs' outstanding guarantees could be quite different. Because those transactions would reduce projected net interest income for the GSEs, they would, under cash accounting, result in a budgetary cost. Moreover, if the expected net rate of return on the portfolio holdings or guarantees exceeded the Treasury borrowing rate, the transactions would, under FCRA accounting, also be reported as having a cost.

Winding Down the GSEs' Operations

Depending on the market structure chosen, policymakers could consolidate some of Fannie Mae's and Freddie Mac's current operations and transfer them to a new or existing federal agency, or they could sell those operations to securitizers in the private sector or liquidate them. Whether the two GSEs were sold as going concerns or were liquidated could affect the price that potential buyers were willing to pay and could have implications for the competitiveness of the private market. Selling the entities as going concerns without federal backing might maximize the price; however, it might also allow successor entities to dominate the secondary market, at least in the short run, which would offset some of the potential gains from increased competition. Indeed, even something as simple as allowing the successor entities to use the names Fannie Mae and Freddie Mac might create the impression that securities issued by the entities were implicitly guaranteed by the federal government, which would distort competition. Thus, policymakers might decide to sacrifice some proceeds from privatization in order to promote a more competitive market structure.

Similar trade-offs arise in considering the appropriate disposition of Fannie Mae's and Freddie Mac's operating assets, such as loan origination and information systems (including automated underwriting systems), data, and the specialized expertise of employees. Under the three market structures with a reduced federal role, the GSEs' assets could be sold to—and their employees hired by— existing or new firms in the secondary market that currently lack the capacity to handle the GSEs' volume of securitization. However, policymakers would need to weigh the benefits and drawbacks from such a sale. For example, some market participants argue that simply selling the GSEs' loan-level performance data to the highest bidder could undermine competition; they advocate making the data freely available to promote competition.[15] Fannie Mae and Freddie Mac also have other nonfinancial assets that could be sold, including their headquarters, regional offices, and equipment.

Managing the GSEs' Existing Financial Assets and Liabilities

A separate issue from how to handle Fannie Mae's and Freddie Mac's current operations is what to do with their accumulated financial assets (such as the MBSs and whole mortgages they hold as investments) and liabilities (such as the payments they will owe in the future on the securities they have issued). The government faces two basic choices for dealing with those assets and liabilities: either retain the GSEs' existing portfolios and guarantees and allow both to diminish as mortgages are paid off, or sell off the portfolios and pay a private entity to assume the guarantee obligations. Whichever structure for the secondary market was ultimately adopted, the expected losses on the GSEs' existing business would largely be borne by taxpayers because private investors would not assume those obligations without adequate compensation.

Investment Portfolios

As of June 30, 2014, Fannie Mae and Freddie Mac had investment portfolios for which the sum of unpaid principal balances on the whole mortgages and MBSs they held totaled about $870 billion (see Figure 4-1). However, the market value of those mortgages is significantly lower than the unpaid principal balances because some of the borrowers are delinquent or in foreclosure (that is, the mortgages are distressed assets). Since the financial crisis, whole mortgages have made up a significantly larger share of the GSEs' portfolios than they did previously because the GSEs have stripped delinquent mortgages from their MBSs (by repurchasing the loans) to meet guarantee obligations. The GSEs' practice of repurchasing delinquent mortgages and placing them in their investment portfolios is likely to continue for the next few years, so eliminating the portfolios while Fannie Mae and Freddie Mac remain in conservatorship is probably not practical.

The revised agreements that Fannie Mae and Freddie Mac reached with the Treasury in 2012 specify that the GSEs must gradually reduce their portfolios of retained mortgages and MBSs. The maximum size of the portfolio that each GSE can keep is scheduled to shrink by 15 percent a year, from $650 billion in December 2012 to $250 billion in December 2018. The agreements with the Treasury also limit the amount of debt securities that the GSEs can issue to finance purchases for their portfolios. (The amount of the two GSEs' outstanding debt roughly corresponds to the size of their portfolios.) Fannie Mae and Freddie Mac are not actively buying new assets for investment, so much of the required reduction in the GSEs' portfolios under current policy can be achieved through natural attrition as mortgages are paid off.

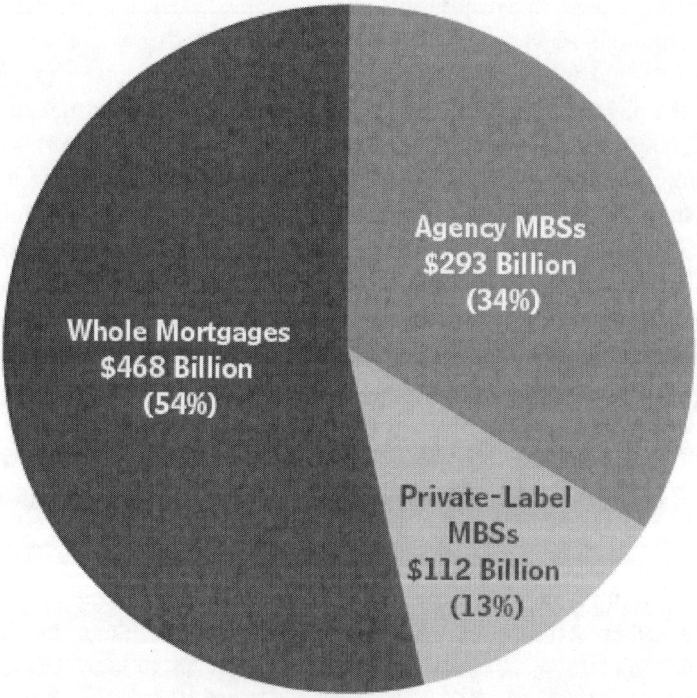

Source: Congressional Budget Office based on data from Fannie Mae and Freddie Mac.

Notes: Agency mortgage-backed securities (MBSs) are issued by federal agencies or government-sponsored enterprises. Private-label MBSs are issued by private companies.

Dollar amounts represent the unpaid principal balance of the mortgages.

Figure 4-1. Fannie Mae and Freddie Mac's Portfolio Holdings of Mortgages and Mortgage-Backed Securities, June 30, 2014.

A decision by policymakers to sell off the GSEs' portfolios more quickly could have various benefits and drawbacks. One benefit is that reducing Fannie Mae's and Freddie Mac's portfolios (and debt) would lower taxpayers' exposure to the risk of larger-than-expected losses and shift responsibility for managing the sold assets to the private sector.[16] But the prices that private investors paid would reflect the compensation that they demanded for bearing that market risk. Selling whole loans to other financial institutions would also be beneficial if those sales improved the process of resolving distressed mortgages and foreclosed properties. The Federal Housing Finance Agency recently announced that Fannie Mae and Freddie Mac will start experimenting with sales of their less-liquid assets (including distressed mortgages but not government-guaranteed MBSs) to test the market. Those sales are likely to cause the GSEs' portfolios to shrink somewhat more quickly than scheduled in the agreements with the Treasury.

One drawback of selling off the GSEs' portfolios quickly is that such sales would generate budgetary costs—but those costs would probably be significant only if the sales occurred in disorderly markets. In particular, selling the portfolio holdings in orderly transactions at market prices would have minimal net budgetary costs on a fair-value basis because the transactions would neither create nor reduce value after adjusting for risk. (Retaining the GSEs' existing portfolios would not result in additional costs or savings to taxpayers unless the fair value of those holdings changed.) However, the transaction costs of such sales would generate small budgetary costs. In addition, accelerating the drawdown of the portfolios to a notable degree would probably generate some costs from distressed sales. For example, if lawmakers set 2016 as a deadline for the GSEs' portfolios to shrink to $250 billion, both Fannie Mae and Freddie Mac would probably need to sell about $50 billion more in assets by that point than they are expected to under current policy. CBO estimates that such sales would have a budgetary cost of about $1 billion because the sales would probably entail selling significant amounts of some relatively illiquid assets at prices below fair value.

More important, if markets were disorderly while sales of portfolio holdings were occurring, the government could incur significant costs on a fair-value basis because value would be lost. Distressed assets, such as nonperforming mortgages and private-label MBSs, could be difficult, and therefore expensive, to sell because buyers lack the information to assess the true worth of those assets. Such assets might be sold only at "fire sale" prices that would be below fair value. But sales of GSEs' holdings of their own

MBSs would probably occur at fair value even in periods of financial distress because they are relatively easy to value.

Changes in Fannie Mae's and Freddie Mac's portfolios would probably have minimal effects on the mortgage and housing markets. Little evidence exists that when the two GSEs purchased each other's or Ginnie Mae's MBSs to hold in their portfolios, any additional savings flowed to mortgage borrowers.[17]

MBS Guarantees

As of June 30, 2014, Fannie Mae's and Freddie Mac's outstanding guarantees together totaled $4.2 trillion as measured by the face value of the underlying mortgages. Disposing of such a large amount of guarantees would be complicated, and the size of the transactions could cause private parties to increase the amount of compensation they required in exchange for assuming those risks. If the government had to pay private investors prices above fair market value to take on all of those obligations—which is likely, given the size of the liabilities—then the transactions would have budgetary costs on a fair-value basis. The government might be able to purchase reinsurance against some of its obligations, just as the GSEs have done in their risk-sharing transactions. However, the government would probably face counterparty risk if the private reinsurers were not able to meet their obligations. In any event, investors in the MBSs would still be relying on the government's guarantee.[18] Consequently, the lowest-cost option for the government might be to retain current guarantees.

APPENDIX: OPTIONS FOR SHIFTING CREDIT RISK TO THE PRIVATE SECTOR

The Federal Housing Finance Agency (FHFA) is encouraging Fannie Mae and Freddie Mac to explore a range of options to shift some of the risk of default on mortgages to the private sector, including issuing mortgage-backed securities (MBSs) without a full guarantee, buying insurance in the form of credit risk notes, and requiring more private mortgage insurance. In response, both of those government-sponsored enterprises (GSEs) undertook multiple risk-sharing transactions in 2013 and 2014 for single-family residential loans.[1] (The two GSEs were already routinely sharing credit risk on mortgages made to owners of multifamily residential properties.) The analysis of risk sharing discussed earlier in this report was based on a generic risk-sharing approach, but different methods of shifting risk to the private sector could have different effects on the secondary mortgage market.

Issue MBSs without a Full Guarantee

Both GSEs could reduce their credit risk by issuing securities without a full guarantee, as Freddie Mac already does with its multifamily MBSs. The cash flows from a pool of mortgages could be segmented into a multiclass—or "senior-subordinate"—structure: Investors holding the senior securities would receive mortgage interest and principal payments before others, whereas those holding the subordinate classes of securities would be first in line to absorb any credit losses. The senior securities, which might be guaranteed by the GSEs, would experience credit losses only after the subordinate securities were wiped out.

Fannie Mae and Freddie Mac would have to pay higher yields on the subordinate MBSs to compensate investors for bearing some of the credit risk. The cost of paying those higher yields would probably be passed on to mortgage borrowers through increases in guarantee fees. Neither GSE has yet used the senior-subordinate structure to share risk on single-family loans, in part because of the expected costs associated with that approach.

Issue Credit Risk Notes

Both Fannie Mae and Freddie Mac have issued debt securities, known as credit risk notes, that function as insurance agreements, effectively insulating the two GSEs from a specified amount of mortgage losses.[2] Those notes are generally sold to investors, such as investment banks, hedge funds, and mutual funds (depending on the structure of the notes). In exchange for periodic payments, investors agree to bear some of the credit risk on a pool of loans or on MBSs. The structure and cash flows of the underlying MBSs are not affected, so such notes do not change the investor base for federally backed ("agency") MBSs.

Payoffs on credit risk notes depend solely on the performance of the designated pool of mortgages or MBSs. If no losses occur on the mortgages or MBSs covered under the agreements, the holders of the notes receive their principal back plus interest. If credit losses are incurred on the mortgages, however, those losses are deducted from the principal amount of the notes. Thus far, to keep interest rates on their credit risk notes low, Fannie Mae and Freddie Mac have retained responsibility for a small initial layer of losses on the pools of loans rather than having investors bear those losses.

Some large banks have used similar notes to share a portion of the credit risk on their holdings of mortgages and private-label MBSs. In addition, property and casualty insurers have used similar structures to share their catastrophic risks with other participants in capital markets.

Before FHFA began pushing for more risk sharing in 2013, the two GSEs had little experience with issuing credit risk notes; Freddie Mac had used a similar structure in 1998 but had not done so since then. The GSEs took several months to issue those notes in 2013 because they first had to grapple with complex tax and accounting questions as well as regulatory requirements and legal issues.

Require More Private Mortgage Insurance

Another option is for Fannie Mae and Freddie Mac to increase their reliance on private mortgage insurance, which is a well-tested approach to shifting credit risk. Borrowers with down payments that are less than the standard required by policymakers—currently 20 percent of a home's purchase price—must purchase insurance from private mortgage insurers who take the first losses on credit defaults (the percentage varies based on the size of the down payment), leaving any excess losses to the two GSEs. For example, if a borrower makes a 10 percent down payment, the private mortgage insurer would generally cover losses up to 25 percent of the original loan amount. Insurers have covered more than $40 billion in credit losses on GSE-backed loans since 2008; over $600 billion in mortgages guaranteed by the GSEs carry private mortgage insurance.

One way to implement that approach is for Fannie Mae and Freddie Mac to buy private mortgage insurance on a pool of loans, as they did in 2013 and 2014.

Alternatively, policymakers could require more borrowers to purchase mortgage insurance from private insurers by raising the standard down payment from 20 percent of a home's purchase price to 30 percent. Or policymakers could retain the 20 percent down payment standard but increase the amount of coverage that mortgage insurance provided for borrowers who lacked the required down payment so that the insurance would provide greater protection against loss of principal. For example, an increase in coverage for a borrower with a 10 percent down payment could mean that a private insurer covers losses up to 35 percent of the principal balance rather than 25 percent of the principal as is required by the GSEs today.

If some borrowers reacted to such an increase in requirements by making bigger down payments to avoid more costly mortgage insurance, the financial system as a whole would face less credit risk. Nevertheless, with such requirements boosting the demand for private mortgage insurance, insurers would have to raise a significant amount of capital to ensure an adequate supply.

Trade-Offs between Those Options

Those three approaches differ in how effectively they would shift credit risk to the private sector. They also vary in how they would affect the liquidity of the secondary mortgage market and the amount of new guarantees made by Fannie Mae and Freddie Mac. FHFA hopes that the GSEs' recent risk-sharing experiments can be scaled up to handle larger volumes in the future and that they will attract a sustainable base of investors.

Effectiveness in Shifting Credit Risk

Credit risk notes are effective in transferring risk because the two GSEs receive investors' payments for the notes up front, which eliminates counterparty risk (the risk that the other party to a transaction defaults and cannot fulfill its obligations).

Partially guaranteed MBSs with a senior-subordinate structure would function much like Freddie Mac's multi-family securities, which are issued without full guarantees. The effectiveness of those MBSs is uncertain and would depend on whether investors assumed that the subordinate classes bore an implicit federal guarantee. (When Fannie Mae and Freddie Mac were placed in conservatorship, the subordinate debt securities they had issued at the corporate level before the financial crisis were protected by such a guarantee. However, investors in the subordinate classes of Freddie Mac's multifamily MBSs were not protected.)

Relying more heavily on private mortgage insurance shifts some of the GSEs' credit risk, but it increases their exposure to counterparty risk. Several private mortgage insurance companies failed during the financial crisis, and some of their costs were borne by the GSEs; other companies had their credit ratings downgraded, indicating that they would have been vulnerable if the crisis had been worse.[3] However, at least one of the GSEs' risk-sharing transactions in 2013 involved an insurer that had no previous exposure to mortgage credit risk. If other insurers who had no previous experience in mortgage insurance entered this segment of the market, they would make more capital available to back private mortgage insurance and could reduce and diversify the government's counterparty risk.

Effectiveness in Maintaining Liquidity

The liquidity of the market for agency MBSs would not be affected by increasing reliance on private mortgage insurance or by the GSEs' issuing credit risk notes. However, liquidity would probably decline if the GSEs issued more securities with incomplete guarantees, which would lead to higher interest rates on mortgages. In particular, MBSs with senior and subordinate classes might be less liquid than the current single-class MBSs if the structure of the new securities did not meet the requirements for trading in the "To Be Announced" (TBA) market for MBSs (a forward market in which lenders promise to deliver in the future a pool of mortgages with preset interest rates that qualify for a federal guarantee).[4]

Currently, the only securities that are eligible to trade in the TBA market are those guaranteed by Fannie Mae, Freddie Mac, or Ginnie Mae; private-label MBSs do not meet TBA standards. Securities that trade in the TBA market are highly standardized and substitutable, which facilitates forward trading because the value of the particular security delivered under a forward agreement should be about the same as any other TBA-eligible security that could be delivered at that date. In contrast, multiclass securities are less homogeneous, and the cash flows received by investors of the senior securities might look different than the cash flows received by investors in TBA-eligible MBSs, so they would be less substitutable, which would complicate forward trades. Preserving the benefits of the TBA market is one of the goals of people who support moving to a hybrid public-private structure for the secondary mortgage market.

Effects on the Volume of New GSE Guarantees

Only one of the risk-sharing mechanisms would directly affect the amount of new guarantees made by Fannie Mae and Freddie Mac (although all three mechanisms would indirectly affect that amount by passing some of the costs of risk sharing on to borrowers in the form of higher guarantee fees). Issuing MBSs without a full guarantee would reduce the volume of new GSE guarantees because the subordinated classes of those securities would not be guaranteed.

End Notes for Summary

[1] Although Fannie Mae and Freddie Mac are now owned and operated by the federal government, CBO still refers to them as GSEs on occasion for simplicity and because significant legal and institutional differences exist between those two entities and fully federal agencies.

[2] For a previous CBO study that examined the strengths and weaknesses of some of those alternative structures as well as the weaknesses of the precrisis model for Fannie Mae and Freddie Mac, see Congressional Budget Office, *Fannie Mae, Freddie Mac, and the Federal Role in the Secondary Mortgage Market* (December 2010), www.cbo.gov/publication /21992.

[3] For additional information, see Congressional Budget Office, letter to the Honorable Barney Frank about the budgetary impact of Fannie Mae and Freddie Mac (September 16, 2010), www.cbo.gov/publication/21707.

End Notes for Section 1

[1] For more information about the securitization process, see Gary Gorton and Andrew Metrick, *Securitization*, Working Paper 18611 (National Bureau of Economic Research, December 2012), www.nber.org/papers/w18611.

[2] An examination of the GSEs' assistance to low- and moderate-income borrowers is beyond the scope of this report. Other federal and state programs also support affordable housing.

[3] Laurie S. Goodman and Jun Zhu, *Reps and Warrants: Lessons From the GSEs Experience* (Urban Institute, Housing Finance Policy Center, October 24, 2013), www.urban 412934.html.

[4] Jerome H. Powell, Member, Board of Governors of the Federal Reserve System, "Thoughts on Unconventional Monetary Policy" (speech given at the Bipartisan Policy Center, Washington, D.C., June 27, 2013), http://go.usa.gov/BdtT (PDF, 54 KB); and Diana Hancock and Wayne Passmore, *How the Federal Reserve's Large-Scale Asset Purchases (LSAPs) Influence Mortgage-Backed Securities (MBS) Yields and U.S. Mortgage Rates*, Finance and Economic Discussion Series Paper 2014-12 (Board of Governors of the Federal Reserve System, February 2014), http://go.usa.gov/BG9R.

[5] Edward J. DeMarco, Acting Director, Federal Housing Finance Agency, "Recent Accomplishments and a Look Ahead at the Future of Housing Finance" (speech given at the Exchequer Club, Washington, D.C., November 28, 2012), http://go.usa.gov/6krY; and Congressional Budget Office, *Modifying Mortgages Involving Fannie Mae and Freddie Mac: Options for Principal Forgiveness* (May 2013), www.cbo.gov/publication/44115.

[6] The $1.9 trillion estimate for mortgage originations in calendar year 2013 comes from *Inside Mortgage Finance*; other sources may show slightly different estimates for the volume of originations and for the GSEs' current market share.

[7] Testimony of Melvin L. Watt, Director, Federal Housing Finance Agency, before the Senate Committee on Banking, Housing, and Urban Affairs, *An Update From the Federal Housing Finance Agency on Fannie Mae, Freddie Mac, and the Federal Home Loan Banks* (November 19, 2014), http://go.usa.gov/6kCT; and Testimony of Edward J. DeMarco, Acting Director, Federal Housing Finance Agency, before the Senate Committee on Banking, Housing, and Urban Affairs, *An Update From the Federal Housing Finance Agency on Oversight of Fannie Mae, Freddie Mac, and the Federal Home Loan Banks* (April 18, 2013), http://go.usa.gov/6kC9.

[8] To enhance liquidity, FHFA is also considering a single security for the two GSEs. See Laurie Goodman and Lewis Ranieri, *Charting the Course to a Single Security* (Urban Institute, September 3, 2014), www.urban

[9] Elizabeth A. Duke, Board of Governors of the Federal Reserve System, "Prescriptions for Housing Recovery" (remarks before the National Association of Realtors Midyear Legislative Meetings and Trade Expo, Washington, D.C., May 15, 2012), http://go.usa.gov/BduV (PDF, 39 KB).

[10] Federal Reserve Board, "The July 2014 Senior Loan Officer Opinion Survey on Bank Lending Practices" (August 4, 2014), http://go.usa.gov/pxbk.

[11] See Congressional Budget Office, *Interest Rate Differentials Between Jumbo and Conforming Mortgages, 1995–2000* (May 2001), www.cbo.gov/publication/13071; and Alex Kaufman, *The Influence of Fannie and Freddie on Mortgage Loan Terms*, Finance and Economics Discussion Series 2012-33 (Board of Governors of the Federal Reserve System, June, 2012), http://go.usa.gov/BdJP.

[12] For the annual projections, see Congressional Budget Office, "Federal Programs That Guarantee Mortgages—April 2014 Baseline" (April 2014), www.cbo.gov/publication /43882. For details about how CBO models the mortgage market and makes its estimates, see Congressional Budget Office, *CBO's Budgetary Treatment of Fannie Mae and Freddie Mac* (January 2010), pp. 15–22, www.cbo.gov/publication/41887. For more information about CBO's budgetary treatment of the two GSEs, see the testimony of Deborah Lucas, Assistant Director for Financial Analysis, Congressional Budget Office, before the House Committee on the Budget, *The Budgetary Cost of Fannie Mae and Freddie Mac and Options for the Future Federal Role in the Secondary Mortgage Market* (June 2, 2011), www.cbo.gov/ publication/41487.

[13] Congressional Budget Office, *Fair-Value Estimates of the Cost of Federal Credit Programs in 2013* (June 2012), www.cbo.gov/ publication/43352.

[14] For a comparison of the GSEs' costs on a fair-value basis and a FCRA basis, see Congressional Budget Office, letter to the Honorable Barney Frank about the budgetary impact of Fannie Mae and Freddie Mac (September 16, 2010), www.cbo.gov/ publication/21707.

[15] For an analysis of the return that taxpayers have received from the GSEs since they were placed in conservatorship, see Larry D. Wall, "Have the Government-Sponsored Enterprises Fully Repaid the Treasury?" *Notes From the Vault* (Federal Reserve Bank of Atlanta, March 2014), www.frbatlanta.org/cenfis/pubscf/ nftv_1403.cfm.

[16] Cash payments from the GSEs reduced the deficit by $74 billion in 2014. That estimate included a $24 billion payment that Freddie Mac made to the Treasury in December 2013 to recognize a revaluation of its deferred tax assets, which was similar to the onetime payment that Fannie Mae made in fiscal year 2013.

[17] Testimony of Deborah Lucas, Assistant Director for Financial Analysis, Congressional Budget Office, before the House Committee on the Budget, *The Budgetary Cost of Fannie Mae and*

Freddie Mac and Options for the Future Federal Role in the Secondary Mortgage Market (June 2, 2011), p. 12, www.cbo.gov/ publication/41487.

[18] For projections of the GSEs' annual loan volumes, subsidy costs, and cash receipts over that period, see Congressional Budget Office, "Federal Programs That Guarantee Mortgages—April 2014 Baseline" (April 2014), www.cbo.gov/publication/43882.

[19] Since CBO completed those projections, the GSEs' average guarantee fee has risen, reaching about 60 basis points in November 2014. Although policymakers have not altered the GSEs' fee schedule, changes in the composition of new GSE guarantees—loans to higher-risk borrowers, which carry higher fees, now make up a slightly larger proportion of those guarantees than they had previously, although loans to lower-risk borrowers still predominate—have caused the average guarantee fee to climb. The increase in receipts due to the higher average fees will, however, be mostly offset by the cost of the increase in expected losses due to the riskier pool of borrowers, so the subsidy rates probably have not changed significantly. Thus, the higher average guarantee fees most likely would not significantly affect CBO's budget estimates.

[20] Neither those projections nor the estimates of the options and transition paths in this report incorporate two recently announced changes in policy. The first will allow the two GSEs to guarantee mortgages with down payments as low as 3 percent of the house price. The previous minimum for most loans was 5 percent. The second requires the two GSEs to begin funding two federal affordable housing programs in 2015, as authorized by the Housing and Economic Recovery Act of 2008. See, respectively, Federal Housing Finance Agency, "Statement of FHFA Director Melvin L. Watt on Release of Guidelines for Purchase of Low Down Payment Mortgages" (press release, December 8, 2014), http://go.usa.gov/FqWm, and "FHFA Statement on the Housing Trust Fund and Capital Magnet Fund" (press release, December 11, 2014), http://tinyurl.com/lxzvfe3.

[21] Federal Reserve, "Federal Reserve Board Approves Final Rule to Help Ensure Banks Maintain Strong Capital Positions" (press release, July 2, 2013), http://go.usa.gov/Bdhm; and Laurie Goodman and others, "New Capital Proposals Applying to Securitizations on Bank Balance Sheets—A Positive Development," *Amherst Mortgage Insight* (Amherst Securities Group, June 15, 2012).

[22] Laurie Goodman and others, "QM: Mortgage Market Implications," *Amherst Mortgage Insight* (Amherst Securities Group, January 16, 2013).

[23] Federal Reserve Board, "The July 2014 Senior Loan Officer Opinion Survey on Bank Lending Practices" (August 4, 2014), http://go.usa.gov/pxbk.

[24] On October 21, 2014, financial regulators announced that they had finalized the credit risk retention rule, but the rule has not yet been published in the *Federal Register*. The announcement and the draft rule are available from the Office of the Comptroller of the Currency, http://go.usa.gov/GXQF. For a critical assessment of the rationales for risk retention, see Paul Willen, "Mandated Risk Retention in Mortgage Securitization: An Economist's View," *American Economic Review*, vol. 104, no. 5 (May 2014), pp. 82– 87, http://dx.doi.org/10.1257/aer.104.5.82.

[25] Earlier versions of the rule would have had more significant effects. See, for example, Federal Reserve Board, *Report to the Congress on Risk Retention* (October 2010), http://go.usa.gov/ Bvqw; and Timothy F. Geithner, *Macroeconomic Effects of Risk Retention Requirements* (Financial Stability Oversight Council, January 2011), http://go.usa.gov/Bvqe (PDF, 202 KB).

[26] Martin S. Hughes, Brett D. Nicholas, and Matthew J. Tomiak, *A Guide To Reviving the Private Label Market* (Redwood Trust, August 2014), http://tinyurl.com/om36ulg; and testimony of

Martin S. Hughes, Chief Executive Officer, Redwood Trust, before the House Committee on Financial Services (April 24, 2013), http://go.usa.gov/Bv3x (PDF, 338 KB).

[27] Christopher B. Killian, Managing Director, Securities Industry and Financial Markets Association, letter to Mary John Miller, Undersecretary for Domestic Finance, Department of Treasury, in response to the Treasury's request for public input on the development of a responsible private label securities market (August 8, 2014), http://go.usa.gov/prF4; and testimony of Chris J. Katopis, Executive Director, Association of Mortgage Investors, before the House Committee on Financial Services (April 24, 2013), http://go.usa.gov/Bv35 (PDF, 521 KB).

[28] For more information about covered bonds and advances from the Federal Home Loan Banks, see Congressional Budget Office, *Fannie Mae, Freddie Mac, and the Federal Role in the Secondary Mortgage Market* (December 2010), pp. 47–49 and 55–56, www.cbo.gov/publication/21992.

End Notes for Section 2

[1] Dwight Jaffee and John M. Quigley, *The Future of the Government Sponsored Enterprises: The Role for Government in the U.S. Mortgage Market*, Working Paper 17685 (National Bureau of Economic Research, December 2011), www.nber.org/papers/ w17685; Philip Swagel, "Increasing the Role of the Private Sector in Housing Finance," in Michael Greenstone and others, eds., *Fifteen Ways to Rethink the Federal Budget* (Hamilton Project, Brookings Institution, February 2013), pp. 76–82, http://tinyurl.com/b8jhys7; and N. Eric Weiss, *Proposals to Reform Fannie Mae and Freddie Mac in the 112th Congress*, Report for Congress R41822 (Congressional Research Service, November 30, 2011).

[2] See, for example, Philip L. Swagel, "The Future of U.S. Housing Finance Reform," *B.E. Journal of Macroeconomics*, vol. 12, no. 3 (October 2012), http://dx.doi.org/10.1515/1935-1690.110.

[3] See, for example, Laurie Goodman and others, *Guarantee Fees—An Art, Not a Science* (Urban Institute, August 14, 2014), www.urban and Mark Zandi and Cristian deRitis, *A General Theory of G-Fees* (Moody's Analytics, October 2014), http://tinyurl.com/ovlyku7 (PDF, 407 KB).

[4] As explained in Section 1 (see footnote 19), although a change in the mix of borrowers caused average guarantee fees to rise to about 60 basis points last summer, that higher average would not significantly affect CBO's budget estimates.

[5] Federal Housing Finance Agency, *Fannie Mae and Freddie Mac Single-Family Guarantee Fees in 2012* (December 2013), http://go.usa.gov/pbzY.

[6] Matthew Jozoff, Nicholas Maciunas, and Jonathan J. Smith, "Agency MBS Outlook," in *2013 Securitized Products Outlook* (U.S. Fixed Income Strategy, J.P. Morgan, November 21, 2012), pp. 3–25.

[7] Testimony of Dwight M. Jaffee, Professor of Banking, Finance and Real Estate, Hass School of Business, University of California at Berkeley, before the Senate Committee on Banking, Housing, and Urban Affairs (September 13, 2011), http://go.usa.gov/Bv4A.

[8] "Agency Share of Jumbo Mortgage Market Expanded Slightly in 2012 as Streamlined Refi Gained Steam," *Inside Mortgage Finance* (March 14, 2013), p. 3, http://tinyurl.com/myo9yyx.

[9] Edward J. DeMarco, Acting Director, Federal Housing Finance Agency, "FHFA's Conservatorship Priorities for 2013" (speech given at the National Association for Business Economics 29th Annual Economic Policy Conference, Washington, D.C., March 4, 2013), http://go.usa.gov/pj7Y.

[10] Pamela Lee and Bing Bai, "Risk Sharing: High-LTV Mortgages are the Next Frontier," *MetroTrends* (blog entry, Urban Institute, May 15, 2014), http://tinyurl.com/n7a63pg.

[11] This approach was taken in the Housing Finance Reform and Taxpayer Protection Act of 2014, S. 1217, 113th Cong. (2014).

[12] If Fannie Mae and Freddie Mac transferred risk by issuing MBSs that did not carry their full guarantees, the volume of new GSE guarantees would decline further, and that decline would increase with the amount of risk being shared. (That additional effect on new guarantees would not occur if Fannie Mae and Freddie Mac transferred risk by requiring borrowers to buy more private insurance or by purchasing insurance against credit losses themselves.) Possible changes in the volume of new GSE guarantees due to that effect are not included in CBO's estimates.

[13] For more on designing such an auction, see Lawrence M. Ausubel and others, "Common-Value Auctions With Liquidity Needs: An Experimental Test of a Troubled-Assets Reverse Auction," in Nir Vulkan, Alvin E. Roth, and Zvika Neeman, eds., *The Handbook of Market Design* (Oxford University Press, 2013), pp. 489–554, http://tinyurl.com/o4dw8ru.

[14] Andrew Davidson and Company, *Modeling the Impact of Housing Finance Reform on Mortgage Rates* (prepared for the Bipartisan Policy Center Housing Commission, January 2013), http://tinyurl.com/ltqp44p (PDF, 212 KB).

[15] James M. Poterba, "Tax Subsidies to Owner-Occupied Housing: An Asset-Market Approach," *Quarterly Journal of Economics*, vol. 99, no. 4 (November 1984), pp. 729–752, http://dx.doi.org/ 10.2307/1883123.

[16] Anthony A. DeFusco and Andrew Paciorek, *The Interest Rate Elasticity of Mortgage Demand: Evidence From Bunching at the Conforming Loan Limit*, Finance and Economics Discussion Series Paper 2014-11 (Board of Governors of the Federal Reserve System, January 2014), http://go.usa.gov/B7uh.

[17] Edward L. Glaeser, Joshua D. Gottlieb, and Joseph Gyourko, "Can Cheap Credit Explain the Housing Boom?" in Edward L. Glaeser and Todd Sinai, eds., *Housing and the Financial Crisis* (University of Chicago Press, 2013), http://tinyurl.com/k2ecu6o; and Manuel Adelino, Antoinette Schoar, and Felipe Severino, *Credit Supply and House Prices: Evidence From Mortgage Market Segmentation,* Working Paper 17832 (National Bureau of Economic Research, February 2012), www.nber.org/papers/ w17832.

[18] William C. Dudley, President, Federal Reserve Bank of New York, "Solving the Too Big to Fail Problem" (remarks at the Clearing House's Second Annual Business Meeting and Conference, New York City, November 15, 2012), http://tinyurl.com/cs8fjsv; and Daniel K. Tarullo, Member, Board of Governors of the Federal Reserve System, "Financial Stability Regulation" (Distinguished Jurist Lecture at the University of Pennsylvania Law School, Philadelphia, October 10, 2012), http://go.usa.gov/BvbG (PDF, 109 KB).

End Notes for Section 3

[1] All of those approaches, except having the government act as guarantor of last resort, were discussed in an earlier CBO report, *Fannie Mae, Freddie Mac, and the Federal Role in the*

Secondary Mortgage Market (December 2010), www.cbo.gov/publication/ 21992. That discussion focused on broad design choices and their implications rather than on the effects of specific policy changes that would lead to the new structures. For another review of various proposals for the secondary mortgage market, see Scott Frame, Larry D. Wall, and Lawrence J. White, *The Devil's in the Tail: Residential Mortgage Finance and the U.S. Treasury*, Working Paper 2012-12 (Federal Reserve Bank of Atlanta, August 2012), www.frbatlanta.org/pubs/wp/12_12.cfm. See also Sean M. Hoskins, N. Eric Weiss, and Katie Jones, *Selected Legislative Proposals to Reform the Housing Finance System*, Report for Congress R43219 (Congressional Research Service, June 11, 2014).

[2] Diana Hancock and Wayne Passmore, "Three Initiatives Enhancing the Mortgage Market and Promoting Financial Stability," *B.E. Journal of Economic Analysis & Policy*, vol. 9, no. 3 (March 2009), http://dx.doi.org/10.2202/1935-1682.2226.

[3] For an analysis of broader criteria, see Government Accountability Office, *Housing Finance System: A Framework for Assessing Potential Changes*, GAO-15-131 (October 2014), www.gao.gov/products/ GAO-15-131.

[4] Under the "severely adverse scenario" stress test that is required under the Dodd-Frank Act, the Federal Housing Finance Agency estimates that the GSEs could require additional federal assistance ranging from $84 billion to $190 billion. See Federal Housing Finance Agency, *Projections of the Enterprises' Financial Performance* (April 30, 2014), http://go.usa.gov/ pjsz.

[5] Mortgage Bankers Association, *Ensuring Liquidity Through a Common, Fungible GSE Security* (May 2013), http://tinyurl.com/ oym3mu6 (PDF, 48 KB).

[6] For examples of recent proposals, see Housing Finance Reform and Taxpayer Protection Act of 2014, S. 1217, 113th Cong. (2014); Congressional Budget Office, cost estimate for S. 1217, the Housing Finance Reform and Taxpayer Protection Act of 2014 (September 5, 2014), www.cbo.gov/publication/45687; White House, "A Better Bargain for the Middle Class: Housing" (fact sheet, August 5, 2013), http://go.usa.gov/BvD3; Housing Commission, Bipartisan Policy Center, *Housing America's Future: New Directions for National Policy* (February 2013), http://tinyurl.com/oh4fskq (PDF, 2.9 MB); Ellen Seidman and others, *A Pragmatic Plan for Housing Finance Reform* (Moody's Analytics, Urban Institute, and Milken Institute, June 19, 2013), www.urban and Laurie S. Goodman, *A Realistic Assessment of Housing Finance Reform* (Urban Institute, August 2014), www.urban.org/publications/ 413205.html.

[7] Diana Hancock and Wayne Passmore, "Catastrophic Mortgage Insurance and the Reform of Fannie Mae and Freddie Mac," in Martin N. Bailey, ed., *The Future of Housing Finance: Restructuring the U.S. Residential Mortgage Market* (Brookings Institution Press, 2011), pp. 111–145, http://tinyurl.com/kd5zjna.

[8] For an alternative approach, see Patricia C. Mosser, Joseph Tracy, and Joshua Wright, *The Capital Structure and Governance of a Mortgage Securitization Utility*, Staff Report 644 (Federal Reserve Bank of New York, October 2013), http://tinyurl.com/p59atqz.

[9] David Scharfstein and Adi Sunderam, "The Economics of Housing Finance Reform," in Martin N. Bailey, ed., *The Future of Housing Finance: Restructuring the U.S. Residential Mortgage Market* (Brookings Institution Press, 2011), pp. 146–198, http:// tinyurl.com/kd5zjna; and Department of the Treasury and Department of Housing and Urban Development, *Reforming America's Housing Finance Market: A Report to Congress* (February 2011), www.treasury.gov/initiatives/Pages/housing

[10] See the Protecting American Taxpayers and Homeowners Act of 2013, H.R. 2767, 113th Cong., http://go.usa.gov/BvuB; and Peter J. Wallison, "Eliminating the GSEs as Part of

Comprehensive Housing Finance Reform," in Martin N. Bailey, ed., *The Future of Housing Finance: Restructuring the U.S. Residential Mortgage Market* (Brookings Institution Press, 2011), pp. 92–110, http://tinyurl.com/kd5zjna.

[11] Congressional Budget Office, *Fannie Mae, Freddie Mac, and the Federal Role in the Secondary Mortgage Market* (December 2010), pp. 47–49, www.cbo.gov/ publication/21992; Dwight M. Jaffee, *Reforming the U.S. Mortgage Market Through Private Market Incentives* (draft, Fisher Center for Real Estate and Urban Economics, University of California at Berkeley, January 31, 2011), http://escholarship.org/ uc/item/4x0357n0; and Dwight Jaffee and John M. Quigley, *The Future of the Government Sponsored Enterprises: The Role for Government in the U.S. Mortgage Market,* Working Paper 17685 (National Bureau of Economic Research, December 2011), www.nber.org/papers/ w17685.

End Notes for Section 4

[1] Andreas Fuster and James Vickery, *Securitization and the Fixed-Rate Mortgage*, Staff Report 594 (Federal Reserve Bank of New York, January 2013), http://tinyurl.com/mjxq4d6.

[2] Emanuel Moench, James Vickery, and Diego Aragon, "Why Is the Market Share of Adjustable-Rate Mortgages So Low?" *Current Issues in Economics and Finance*, vol. 16, no. 8 (Federal Reserve Bank of New York, December 2010), http://tinyurl.com/ n3mmrru.

[3] Rates would rise further during the transitions if policymakers increased capital requirements for banks and guarantors or imposed additional fees to fund affordable housing initiatives.

[4] The effects on demand from the interest rate changes during a transition might be relatively small. See Anthony A. DeFusco and Andrew Paciorek, *The Interest Rate Elasticity of Mortgage Demand: Evidence From Bunching at the Conforming Loan Limit*, Finance and Economics Discussion Series Paper 2014-11 (Federal Reserve Board, January 15, 2014), http://go.usa.gov/6PUz.

[5] Mark Zandi and Cristian deRitis, *Housing Finance Reform Steps Forward* (Moody's Analytics, March 2014), http://tinyurl.com/ nw4unfr (PDF, 330 KB), and *The Future of the Mortgage Finance System,* Special Report (Moody's Analytics, February 7, 2011), http://tinyurl.com/ndlqd93 (PDF, 902 KB); and Philip Swagel, *Reform of the GSEs and Housing Finance,* White Paper (Milken Institute, July 2011), www.milkeninstitute.org/ publications/view/464.

[6] Hui Shan and Sven Jari Stehn, *US House Price Bottom in Sight*, Global Economics Paper 209 (Goldman Sachs, December 15, 2011).

[7] Benjamin H. Harris, *The Effect of Proposed Tax Reforms on Metropolitan Housing Prices* (Urban Institute and Brookings Institution Tax Policy Center, April 2010), http://tinyurl.com/ qzgjyuu (PDF, 220 KB).

[8] Ron J. Feldman, "Mortgage Rates, Homeownership Rates, and Government-Sponsored Enterprises," *The Region*, Federal Reserve Bank of Minneapolis, vol. 16, no. 1 (April 2002), pp. 5–23, http://tinyurl.com/k5wuzy2. Moreover, other aspects of government policy affect borrowers more significantly than does the magnitude of guarantee fees. For example, the subsidies that are provided by the tax treatment of home ownership are significantly larger than those that flow through the two GSEs— although those subsidies are also largely capitalized in house prices. For a related discussion, see Larry Ozanne, *Taxation of Owner-*

Occupied and Rental Housing, Working Paper 2012-14 (Congressional Budget Office, November 2012), www.cbo.gov/ publication/43691.

[9] Deborah J. Lucas, "First Discussant Comment on 'The Future of U.S. Housing Finance Reform,'" *B.E. Journal of Macroeconomics*, vol. 12, no. 3 (October 2012), article 12, http://dx.doi.org/ 10.1515/1935-1690.111.

[10] For example, the Mortgage Bankers Association has a monthly index that tracks the magnitude of changes in mortgage credit conditions based on loan and borrower characteristics. See Mortgage Bankers Association, "Mortgage Credit Availability Index," www. mortgagebankers.org/ResearchandForecasts/ mcai.htm.

[11] Because Ginnie Mae securitizes almost all mortgages insured by FHA, its securitizations would rise by a similar amount.

[12] Congressional Budget Office, "How FHA's Mutual Mortgage Insurance Fund Accounts for the Cost of Mortgage Guarantees," *CBO Blog* (October 22, 2013), www.cbo.gov/ publication/44634.

[13] See, for example, the Protecting American Taxpayers and Homeowners Act of 2013, H.R. 2767, 113th Cong., http://go.usa.gov/BvuB; and Congressional Budget Office, cost estimate for H.R. 2767, the Protecting American Taxpayers and Homeowners Act of 2013 (October 28, 2013), www.cbo.gov/ publication/44672.

[14] Congressional Budget Office, *Budgetary Estimates for the Single-Family Mortgage Guarantee Program of the Federal Housing Administration* (September 2014), www.cbo.gov/ publication/ 45740; Francesca Castelli and others, *Modeling the Budgetary Costs of FHA's Single Family Mortgage Insurance*, Working Paper 2014-05 (Congressional Budget Office, September 11, 2014), www.cbo.gov/publication/45711; Congressional Budget Office, "FHA's Single-Family Mortgage Guarantee Program: Budgetary Cost or Savings?" *CBO Blog* (October 21, 2013), www.cbo.gov/ publication/44628, and *Accounting for FHA's Single-Family Mortgage Insurance Program on a Fair-Value Basis* (attachment to a letter to the Honorable Paul Ryan, May 18, 2011), www.cbo.gov/ publication/41445.

[15] See, for example, the letter from John A. Courson and Michael D. Berman, Mortgage Bankers Association, to Alfred M. Pollard, General Counsel, Federal Housing Finance Agency (September 7, 2010), http://tinyurl.com/q8dc5by (PDF, 78 KB).

[16] Robert A. Eisenbeis, W. Scott Frame, and Larry D. Wall, "An Analysis of the Systemic Risks Posed by Fannie Mae and Freddie Mac and an Evaluation of the Policy Options for Reducing Those Risks," *Journal of Financial Services Research*, vol. 31, no. 2–3 (June 2007), pp. 75–99, http://dx.doi.org/10.1007/ s10693-006-0002-z.

[17] Andreas Lehnert, Wayne Passmore, and Shane M. Sherlund, "GSEs, Mortgage Rates, and Secondary Market Activities," *Journal of Real Estate Finance and Economics*, vol. 36, no. 3 (April 2008), pp. 343–363, http://dx.doi.org/10.1007/s11146- 007-9047-5.

[18] Steven G. Bradbury, Principal Deputy Assistant Attorney General, letter to the Secretary of the Treasury, *Enforceability of Certain Agreements Between the Department of the Treasury and Government Sponsored Enterprises* (September 26, 2008), http://go.usa.gov/ 6VuQ (PDF, 295 KB).

End Notes for Appendix

[1] See the testimonies of Laurel Davis, Vice President, Fannie Mae, and Kevin Palmer, Vice President, Freddie Mac, before the Senate Committee on Banking, Housing, and Urban Affairs (December 10, 2013), http://go.usa.gov/BvJx.

[2] Credit risk notes are conceptually similar to another type of debt called credit-linked notes, but the two have different legal structures. Whereas credit risk notes can be issued directly by Fannie Mae and Freddie Mac, credit-linked notes would have to be issued indirectly, through special-purpose entities. Credit-linked notes also present more complex regulatory, tax, and accounting issues than do credit risk notes.

[3] Mark M. Zandi, Jim Parrott, and Cristian deRitis, *Putting Mortgage Insurers on Solid Ground* (Urban Institute/Moody's Analytics, August 2014), www.urban 413213.html; Jeremy Rosenbaum, Ron A. Joas, and Saurabh B. Khasnis, *Will the Sea Change in Lending Standards Be Enough to Buoy U.S. Mortgage Insurers?* (Standard & Poor's, October 8, 2012); and Ron A. Joas and others, *U.S. Mortgage Insurer Sector Outlook Remains Negative—And the Clock's Ticking* (Standard & Poor's, March 1, 2012).

[4] James Vickery and Joshua Wright, "TBA Trading and Liquidity in the Agency MBS Market," *Economic Policy Review,* Federal Reserve Bank of New York, vol. 19, no. 1 (May 2013), pp. 1–18, http://tinyurl.com/qfbfvhp; and testimony of Andrew Davidson, President, Andrew Davidson & Co., before the Subcommittee on Securities, Insurance, and Investment of the Senate Committee on Banking, Housing, and Urban Affairs, *Examining the Housing Finance System: The To-Be-Announced Market* (August 3, 2011), http://go.usa.gov/BvhR (PDF, 253 KB).

INDEX

D

E

F

Q

R

S